THEN & NOW

SNOW HILL

OPPOSITE: Chanceford Hall was built between 1759 and 1792 and has changed hands and names numerous times. The original plot of land was said to be 35 acres of farmland owned by James Rowand Morris. Chanceford Hall's previous names include Chanceford, Boxhaul, Ingleside, Tingle's Place, and Stanton Home. Chanceford Hall has 10 working fireplaces, 7 bathrooms, 6 bedrooms, a formal living area, a formal dining area that was once a ballroom, a two-story kitchen, and a solarium addition. There is a full basement and attic space on either side of the home's third floor, with one side used as the sixth bedroom. (Courtesy of the Worcester County Library.)

THEN & NOW

SNOW HILL

Michelle C. Fulton
and Missy Lunsford

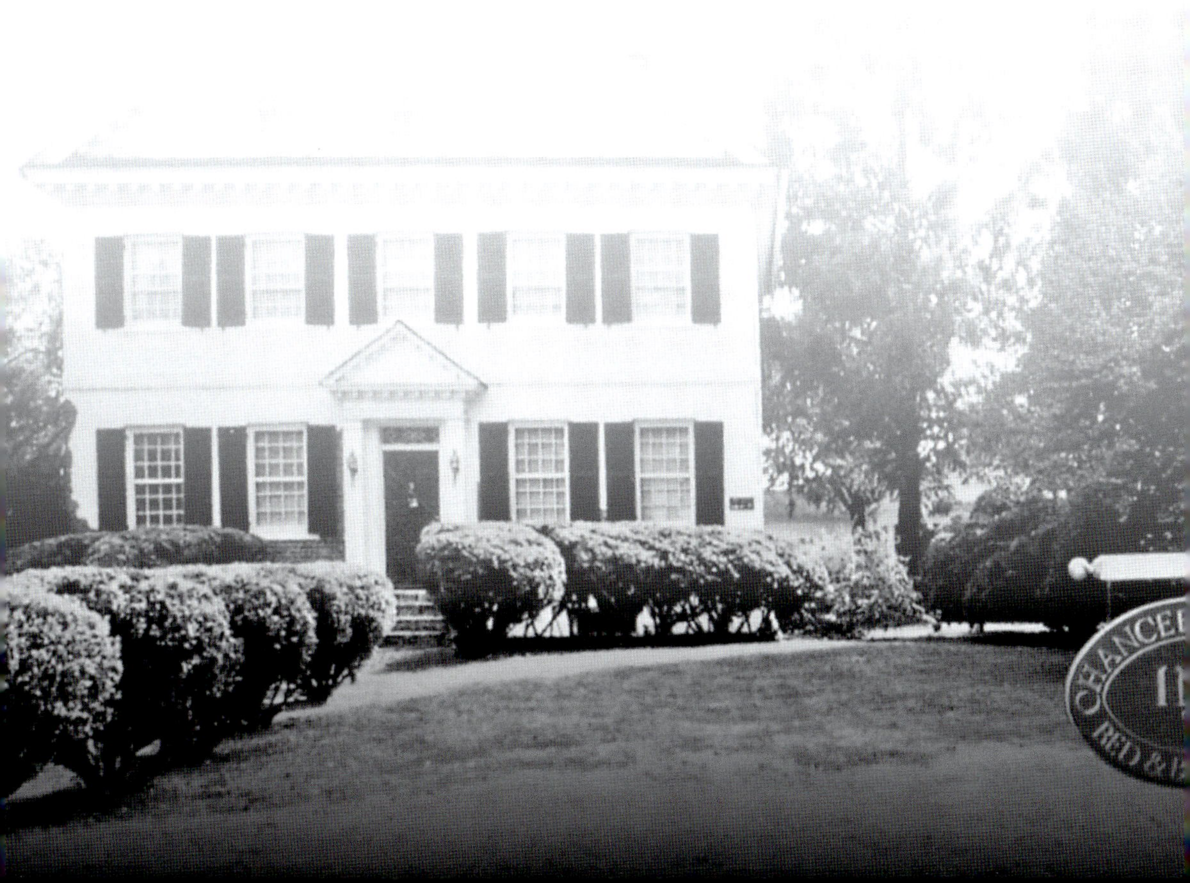

I would like to dedicate this book to all who believed in me,
even when it was hard to believe in myself.
Old friends, new friends, and family,
you all had a part in my success story.
Thank you. This book is for you.

—Michelle C. Fulton

ISBN 978-0-7385-5431-0

Library of Congress control number: 2008923479

Published by Arcadia Publishing
Charleston SC, Chicago IL, Portsmouth NH, San Francisco CA

Printed in the United States of America

For all general information contact Arcadia Publishing at:
Telephone 843-853-2070
Fax 843-853-0044
E-mail sales@arcadiapublishing.com
For customer service and orders:
Toll-Free 1-888-313-2665

Visit us on the Internet at www.arcadiapublishing.com

On the Cover: Located on West Market Street in Snow Hill, the Julia A. Purnell Museum houses a wealth of history and information for all to enjoy. Additional information on the history is located in chapter one.

Contents

Acknowledgments

First and foremost, I would like to thank the Worcester County Library and Rob (Charles) Hall for the many hours of time, knowledge, and resources that were given. Rob (Charles) Hall ran copies back and forth when I couldn't leave work and shared an undeniable wealth of history.

Thank you to the Business Center for doing what didn't seem possible in the time I allowed for picture production and bearing with me through the cranky phone calls I frequently made. Thank you to the Julia A. Purnell Museum for lending me pictures I desperately needed to complete this book.

Andy Nunez, author and friend, thank you for the Friday you spent with me getting things together for my deadline and the wise advice you shared that got me on track. Melissa D. Lunsford, my lifelong friend, this book wouldn't have been possible without your help. The endless hours we spent doing research, naming titles, and basically laughing at each other made this possible. Thank you for being my friend. I am forever grateful.

A special thank-you to my parents for telling the whole world that their daughter was writing a book. I thank you for all you have done for me from my childhood until now; without your support on this project, it would have been near impossible. Evermore thanks. My dear friend Linda Hillard, thank you for all your time and effort in the last stages of my book. Your help meant a great deal to me, given that your home had just burnt down a few days earlier. You didn't have the time, but you made it for me when I needed it the most, and that's what a true friend does. Thank you. To Eric C. Waidner, thank you for your love and support throughout this process. Your unwillingness to let me quit when this book became difficult got me through, and your smile and love are forever in my heart. Thank you for being the rock that kept me together. I love you.

And last but certainly not least, thanks to the town of Snow Hill and to all whom I received stories from, Huey Brown for the newspaper collection and wise words, Shirley McWilliams for the milk factory information, and the Bishop family for the stories about the Moore Lumber Company.

Becoming a published photographer and author has been a dream of mine since elementary school—thank you all for your encouraging words and helpful stories!

Introduction

Snow Hill was founded by English settlers in 1686. It is said that the name of this great town came from the small neighborhood in London called Snow Hill. The town received its first charter on October 26, 1686, and was made a port of entry in 1694. Snow Hill was part of Somerset County until 1742 and was then carved out into Worcester County and named the county seat. Trade was said to be the engine that drove commerce in the town, and the Pocomoke River was dubbed the highway that made import and export possible. Snow Hill became known as a town of gracious living to merchants, bankers, farmers, and sea captains. It was also a fine place for craft specialists who became successful due to the town's navigable river.

In 1883, a fire destroyed most of the commercial area of Snow Hill, including, but not limited to, the courthouse, hotels, and much-needed businesses. Within the next two years, all of the buildings were reconstructed.

Today the downtown area is home primarily to historic buildings with architectural designs of the late 19th century. A tour of the town through this pictorial time line shows the past and the present, and brings in a little of the future of this quaint little town that many call home.

Snow Hill was once home to John Walter Smith, congressman for Maryland's 1st District and the state's 44th governor. From 1907 through 1919, John Walter Smith served as a U.S. senator. He was born in Snow Hill on February 5, 1845. Today there is a park named in his memory on the beautiful banks of the Pocomoke River. Snow Hill was home to many other notable people. Julia A. Purnell is definitely one of the notable people who graces the town with their presence. Ephraim King Wilson II, a U.S. senator and congressman for Maryland's 1st District, was born in Snow Hill on December 22, 1821.

Then & Now: *Snow Hill* is a pictorial history book that was written with the intention of sharing the town's hidden beauty with the public.

CHAPTER 1

Julia A. Purnell Remembered

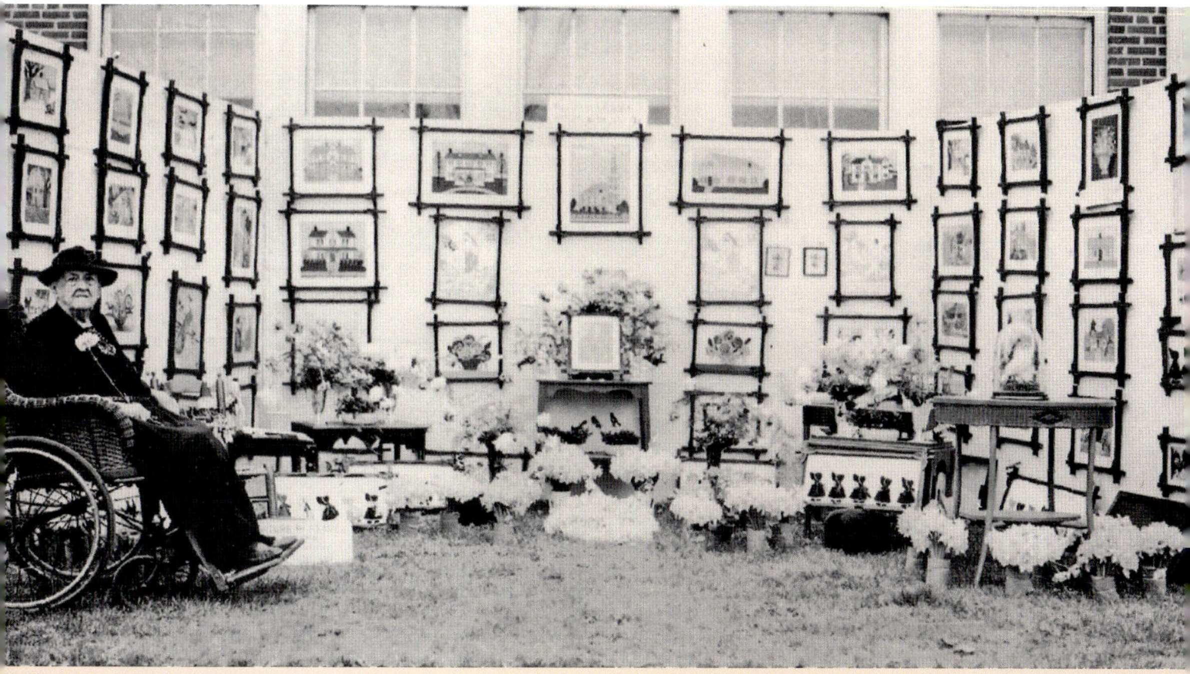

Julia Anne Lecompte was born in Snow Hill in 1843. She married storekeeper William H. Purnell in 1869 and had two sons. Julia was a very active woman, even after a fall at 85 left her in a wheelchair. To occupy her time, she took up needlework, mostly of historic sites around Snow Hill. She won the New York and Philadelphia hobby shows and took the grand prize at the Wicomico Farm and Home Show. Her artwork became well known, and she received encouraging letters from all over the world, including one from Pres. Franklin D. Roosevelt and his wife, Eleanor. In 1941, Julia was inducted into the Hobby Hall of Fame. (Courtesy of Julia A. Purnell Museum.)

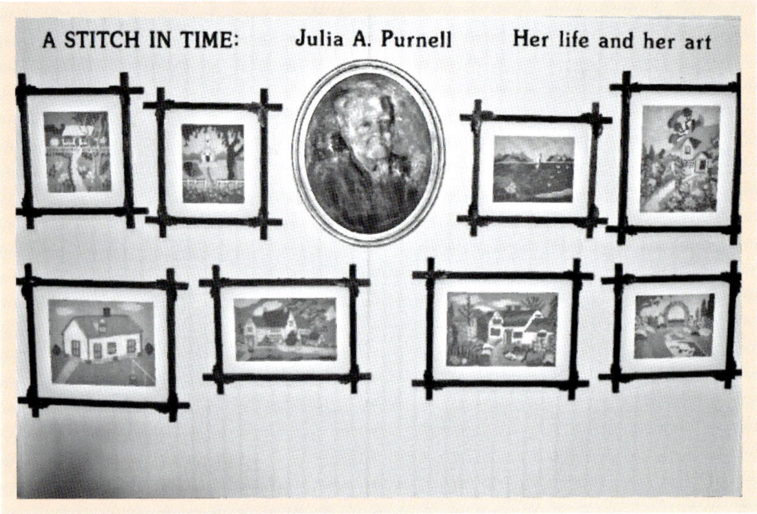

Julia A. Purnell was injured in a fall and left wheelchair-bound at 85. As a hobby, Julia started to needlework pictures of historic sites in town. Her son William made oak frames with oak leaves in the corners to compliment her work. Today Julia's framed needlework is highly sought after and can be seen at the Purnell Museum on West Market Street. Art lives in Snow Hill and continues to grow with monthly art shows at local galleries. Julia A. Purnell left a legacy of art and achievement. (Then photograph courtesy of Purnell Museum; now photograph by the author.)

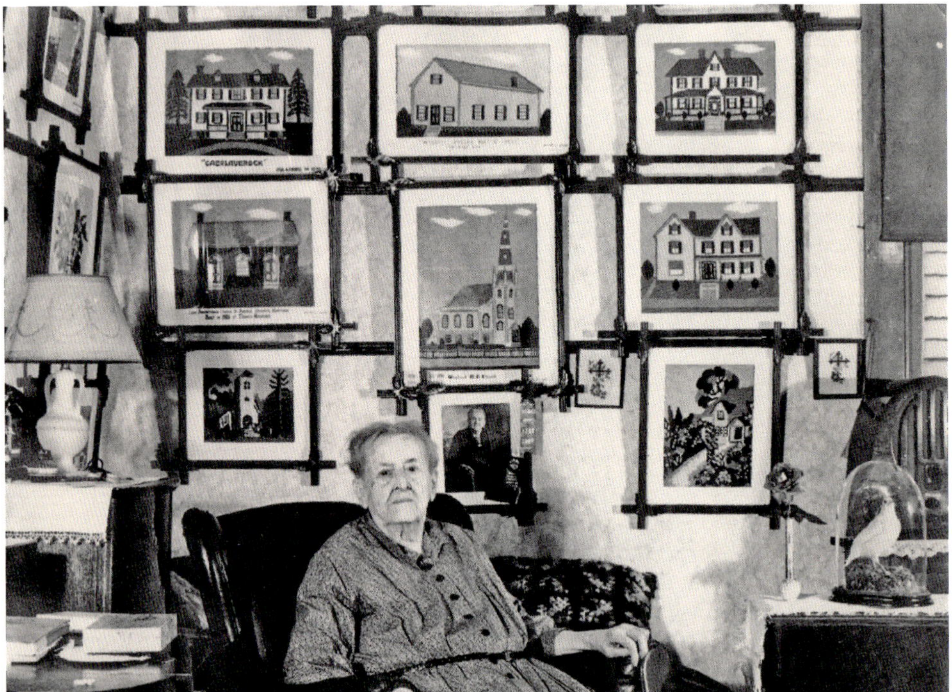

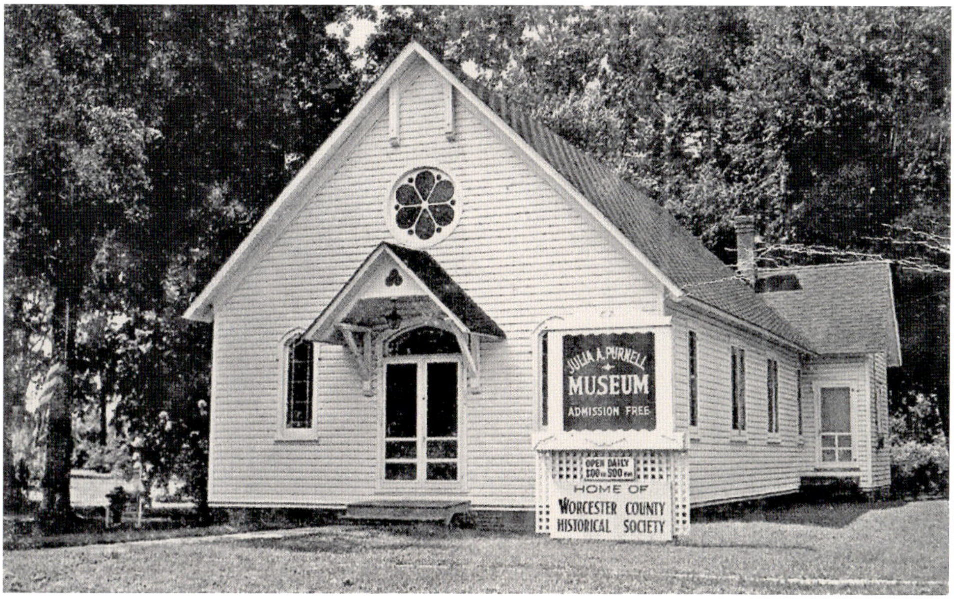

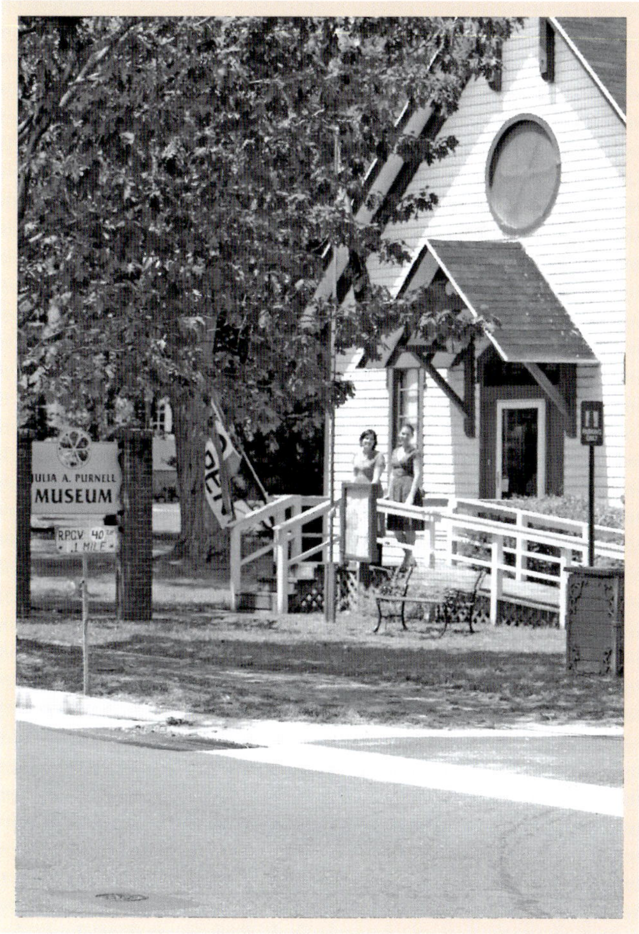

Built in 1891, the Purnell Museum building was originally a Catholic church in the Wilmington archdiocese, but it was never successful. The church closed early in the 20th century, and the building housed public meetings and functions. In 1957, the Julia A. Purnell Museum was founded by son William Purnell and Julia A. Purnell. The Purnell Museum was turned over to the town to keep the heritage going. Today the museum offers history to visitors in interpretive exhibits depicting the lives of Snow Hill and Worcester Countians. (Then photograph courtesy of Purnell Museum; now photograph by the author.)

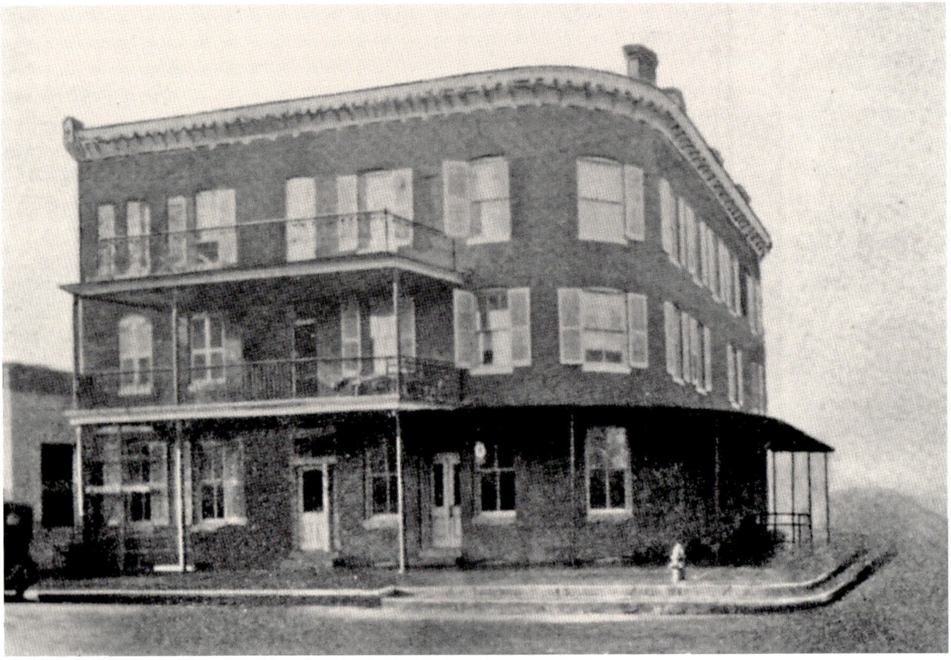

The Purnell Hotel, owned by the Purnell family, was located on the corner of West Green and North Washington Streets. This three-story building stood for more than 70 years before it was knocked to the ground. Now the office building for the Tri-County Council is located in its place. The site was once home to the Edgehill Pharmacy. (Then photograph courtesy of Worcester County Library; now photograph by the author.)

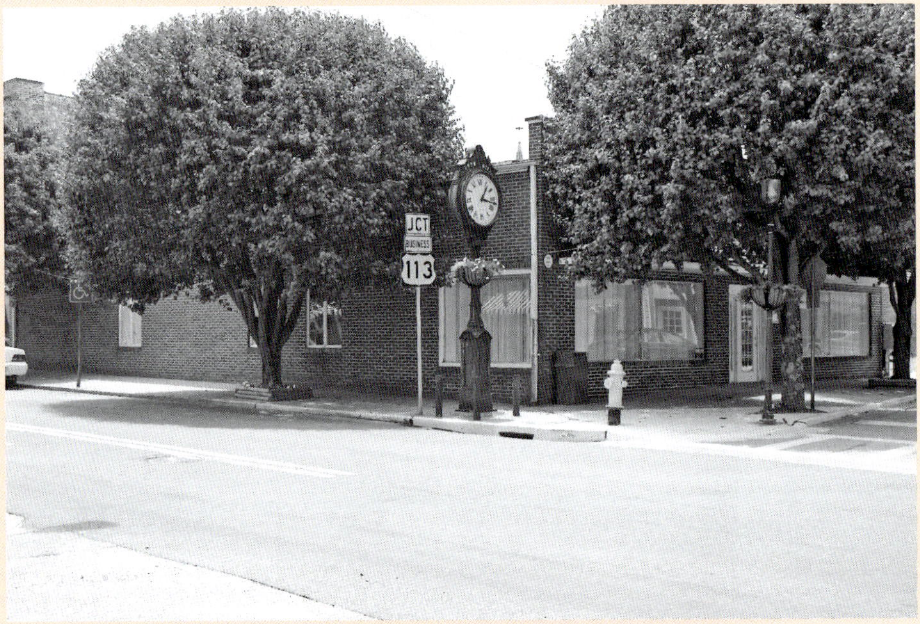

CHAPTER 2

Rest Easy on the Pocomoke

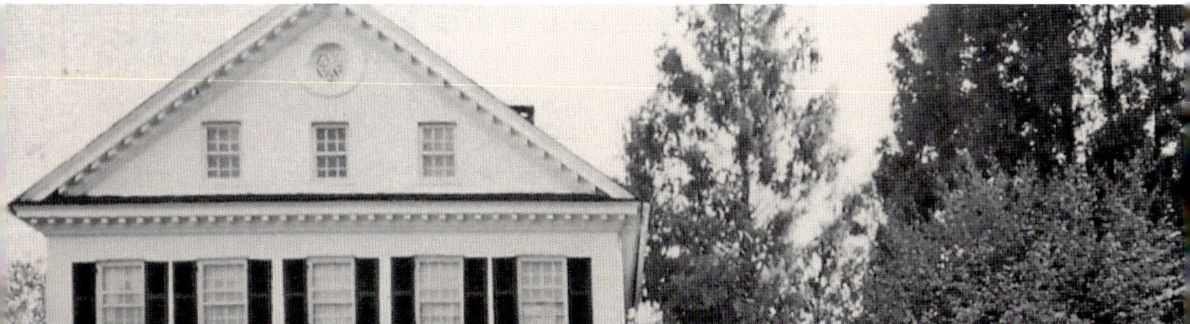

During the past two centuries, Chanceford Hall has, like many historic homes in Snow Hill, had numerous owners and names. Chanceford Hall's original name was Boxhaul, followed by Ingleside, Chanceford, and the Stanton Home. Now the stately home is run as a bed-and-breakfast. The current owner is architect Randy Ifft from Chicago. (Courtesy of Worcester County Library.)

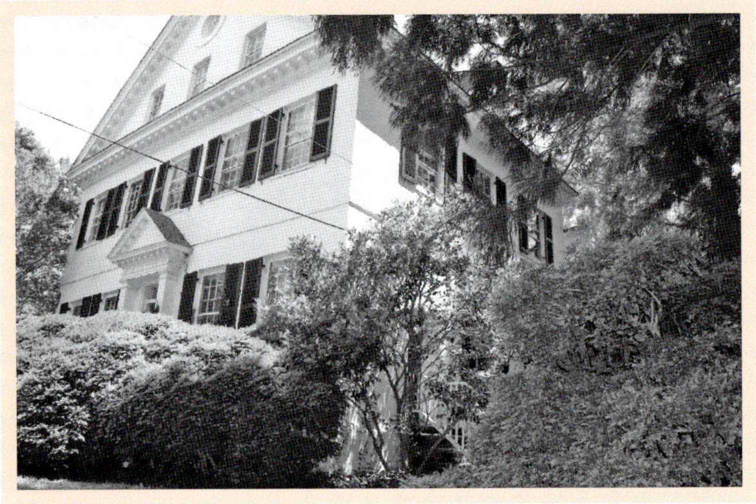

Chanceford Hall is known for it massive chimneys, which are accompanied by 10 working fireplaces. The grounds around the home are similar to how they were in the early years. Now beautiful gardens, bamboo, boxwoods, and magnolia trees surround the home. (Then photograph courtesy of Worcester County Library; now photograph by the author.)

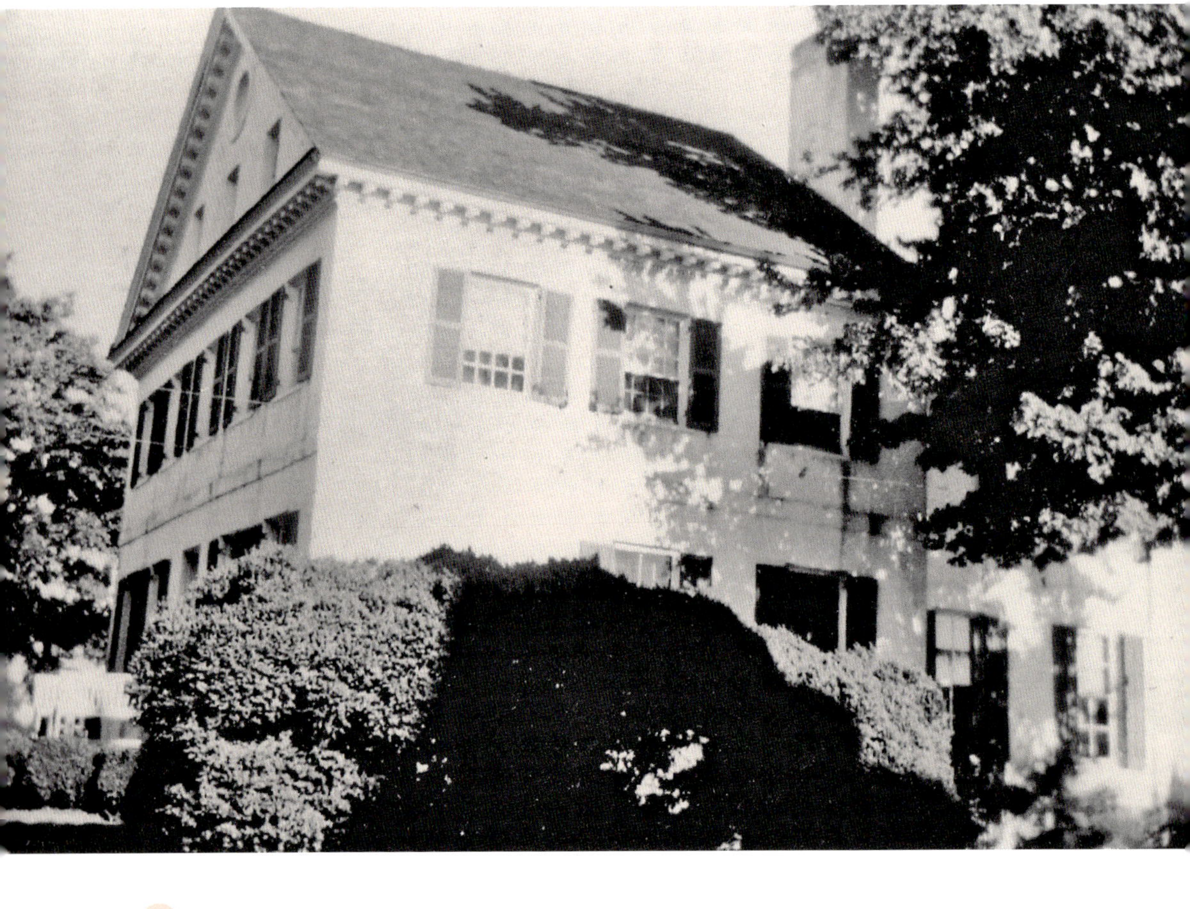

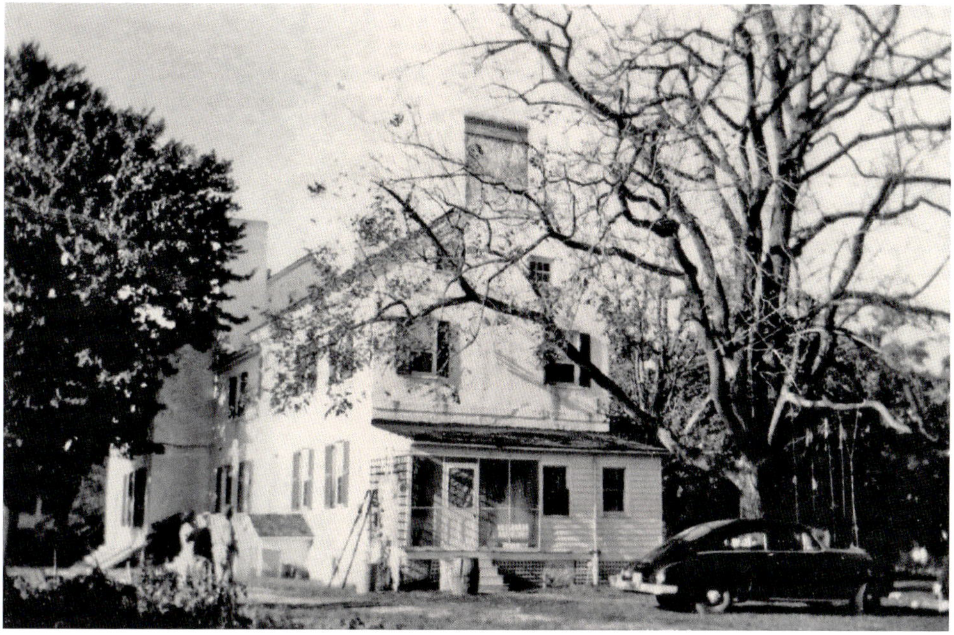

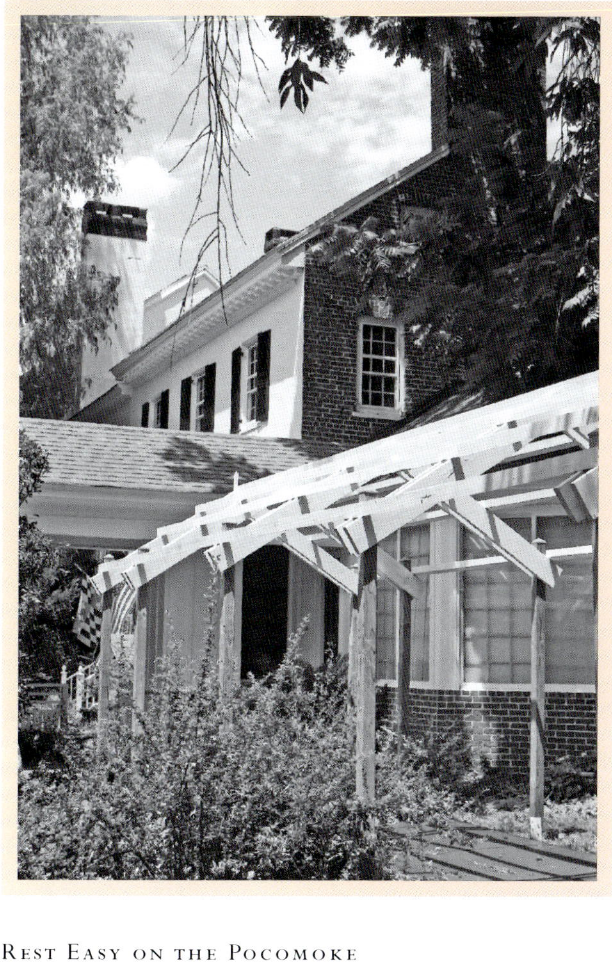

The back of Chanceford Hall once had stairs that led to an entryway; today the back of the house has been expanded with a solarium, a lap pool, and a lofted garage. The chimneys and third-floor windows remain. (Then photograph courtesy of Worcester County Library; now photograph by the author.)

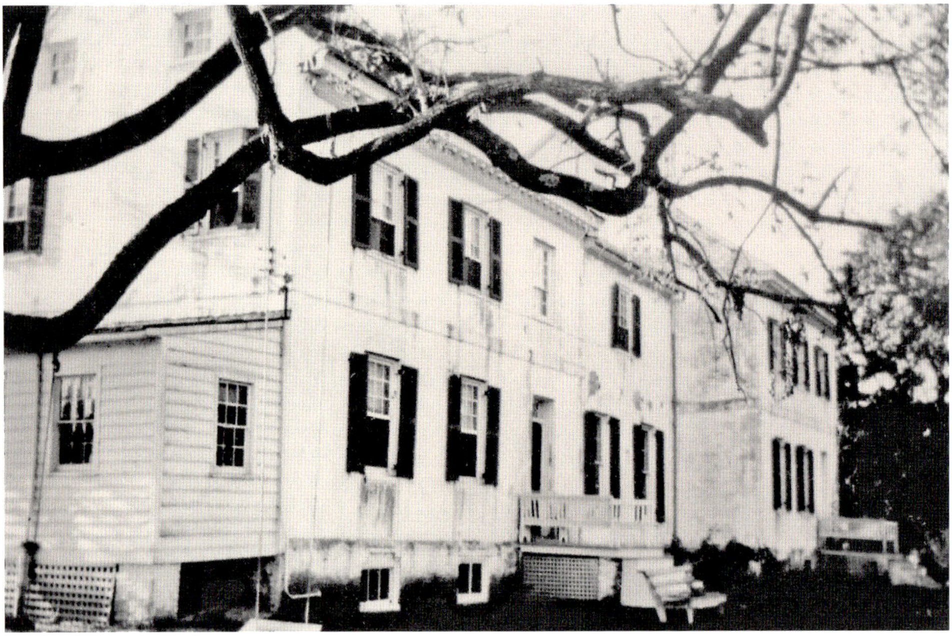

The basement windows are visible, along with the two, small, entryway platforms. The original brick is exposed, and without a doubt, it was built well. Now the back left side of this home has a large deck and has been landscaped. The large tree is still standing. (Then photograph courtesy of Worcester County Library; now photograph by the author.)

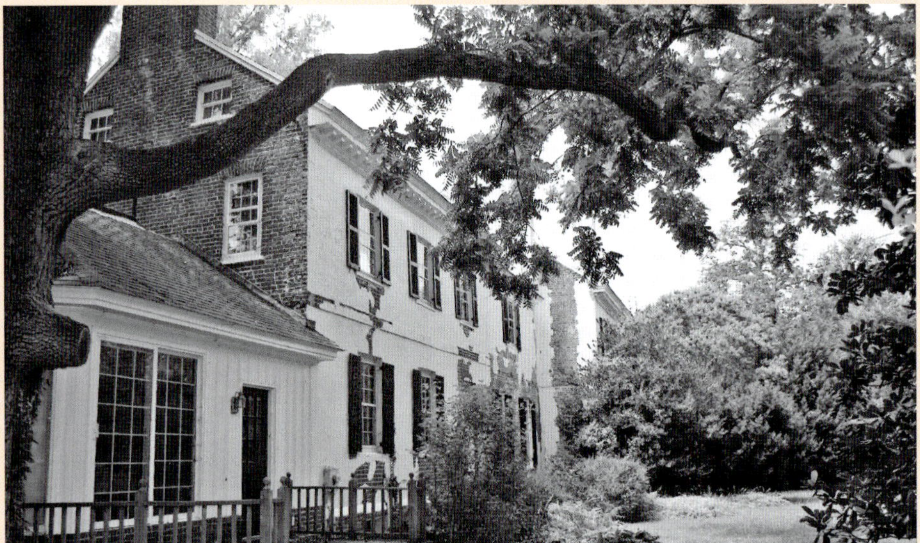

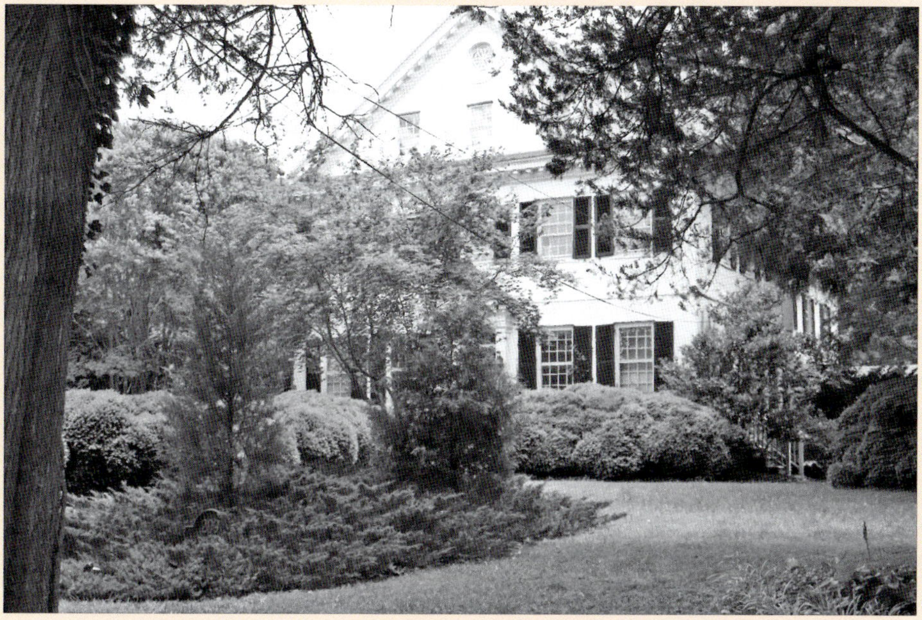

Below is a rare picture of Chanceford showing a dirt driveway, a front screened porch, and various planted trees. Now the front porch is no longer attached, the driveway has been paved and lined with growth, and boxwoods line a concrete sidewalk to the red front door. (Then photograph courtesy of the Worcester County Library; now photograph by the author.)

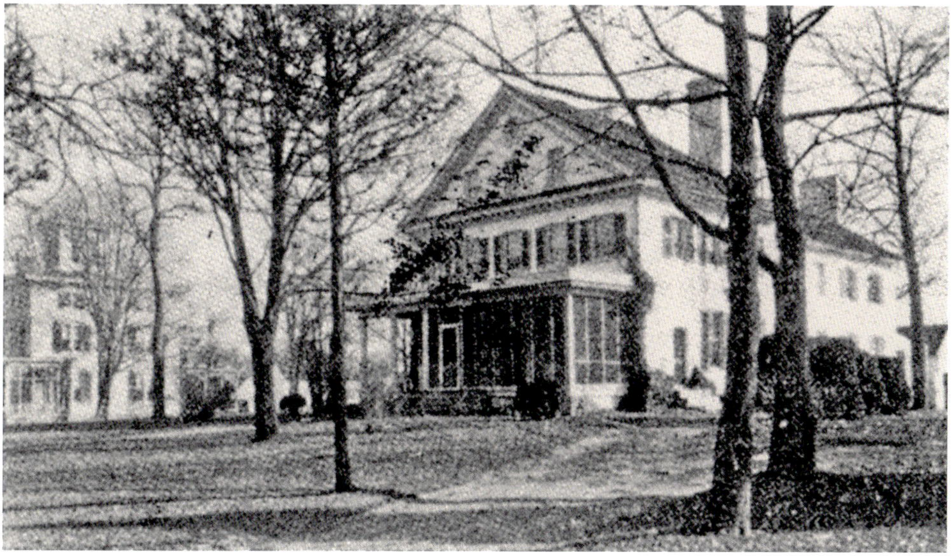

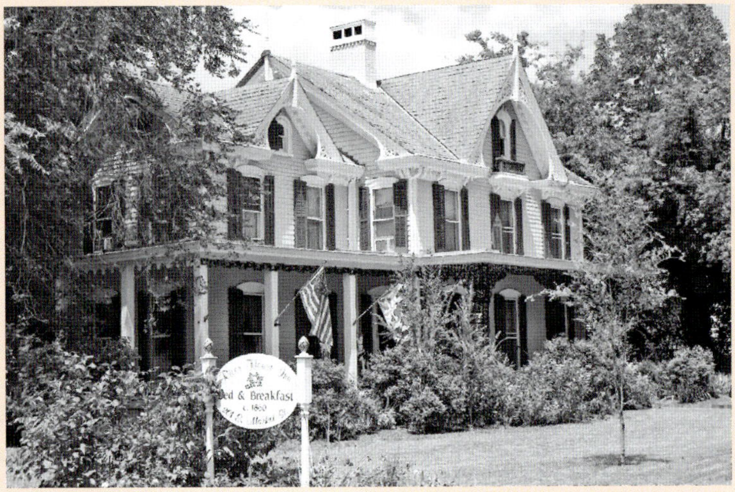

The *c.* 1860 River House Inn was built by George W. P. Smith, who purchased the land from Samuel and Elizabeth Johnson. George Smith lost the home to the court, and George S. and Lelia Payne purchased it for $2,758. The home was named Maples by George W. Purnell in 1899. The home was sold out of the family in 1975. Now the River House Inn is run and owned by Larry and Susanne Knudsen as a bed-and-breakfast. (Then photograph courtesy of Worcester County Library; now photograph by the author.)

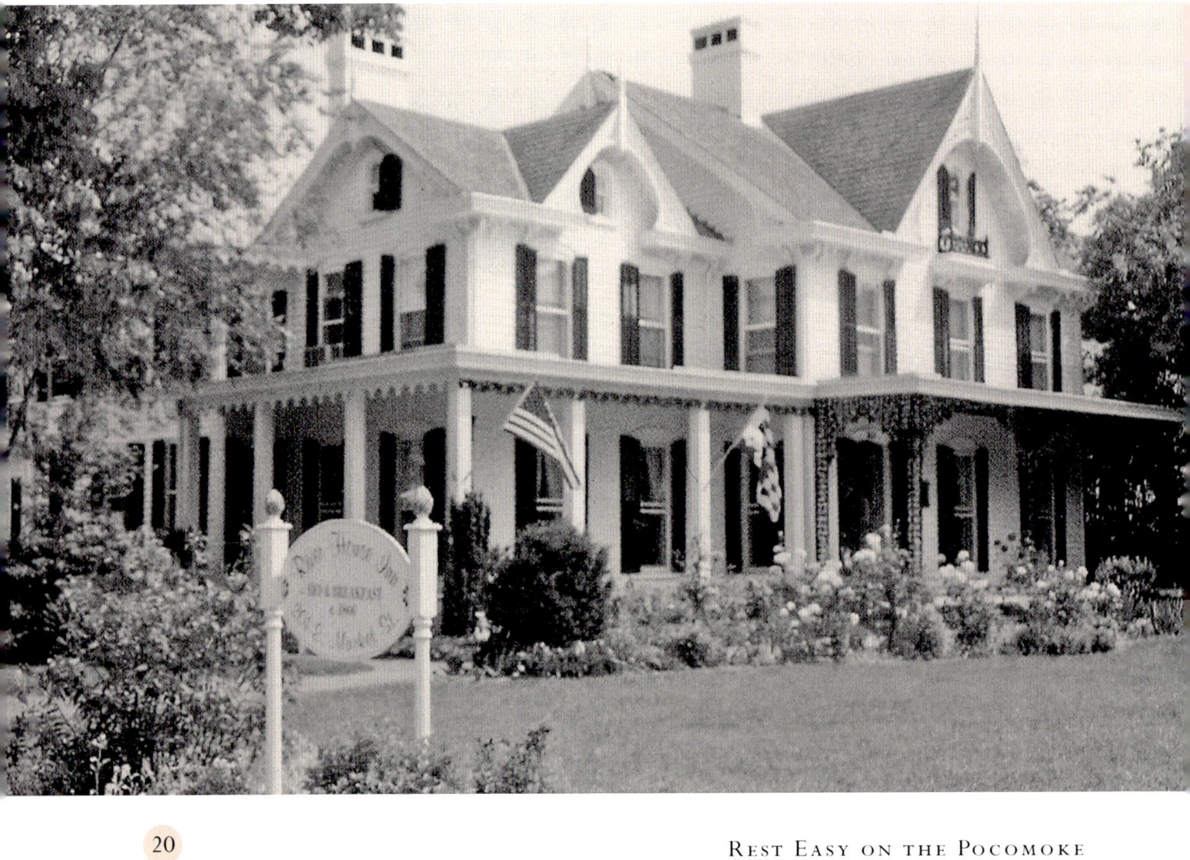

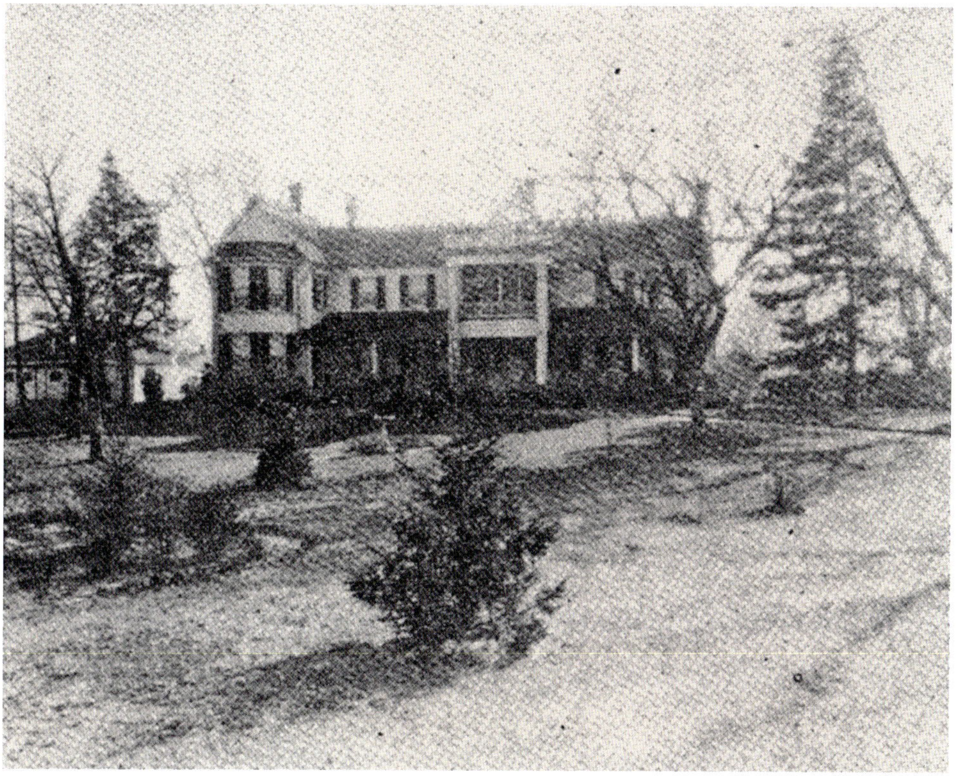

The Walter P. Snow house is located on Federal Street and was built in 1850. The home is a two-story T-shaped house. The original kitchen was in a separate building on the property behind the home. Now the Cedars, as it is known, is owned by Doug and Sherry Willcox and is run as a bed-and-breakfast. The building is currently under construction, and when completed, it will have a second floor wraparound terrace that will serve as a fire exit. (Then photograph courtesy of Worcester County Library; now photograph by the author.)

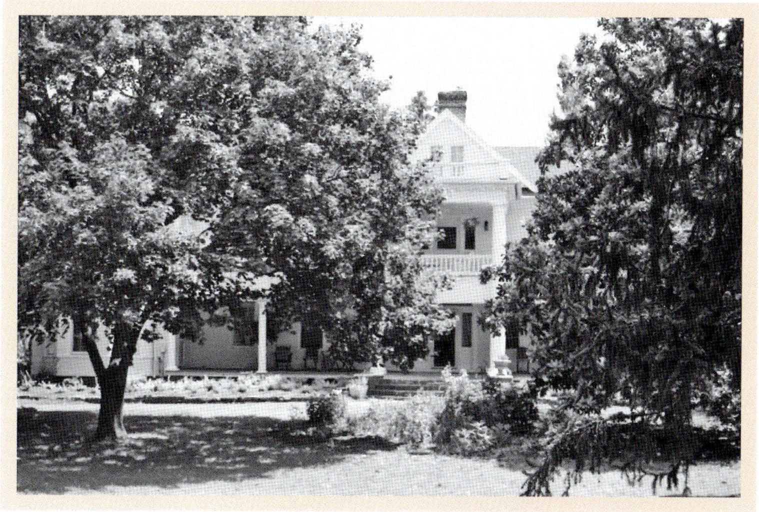

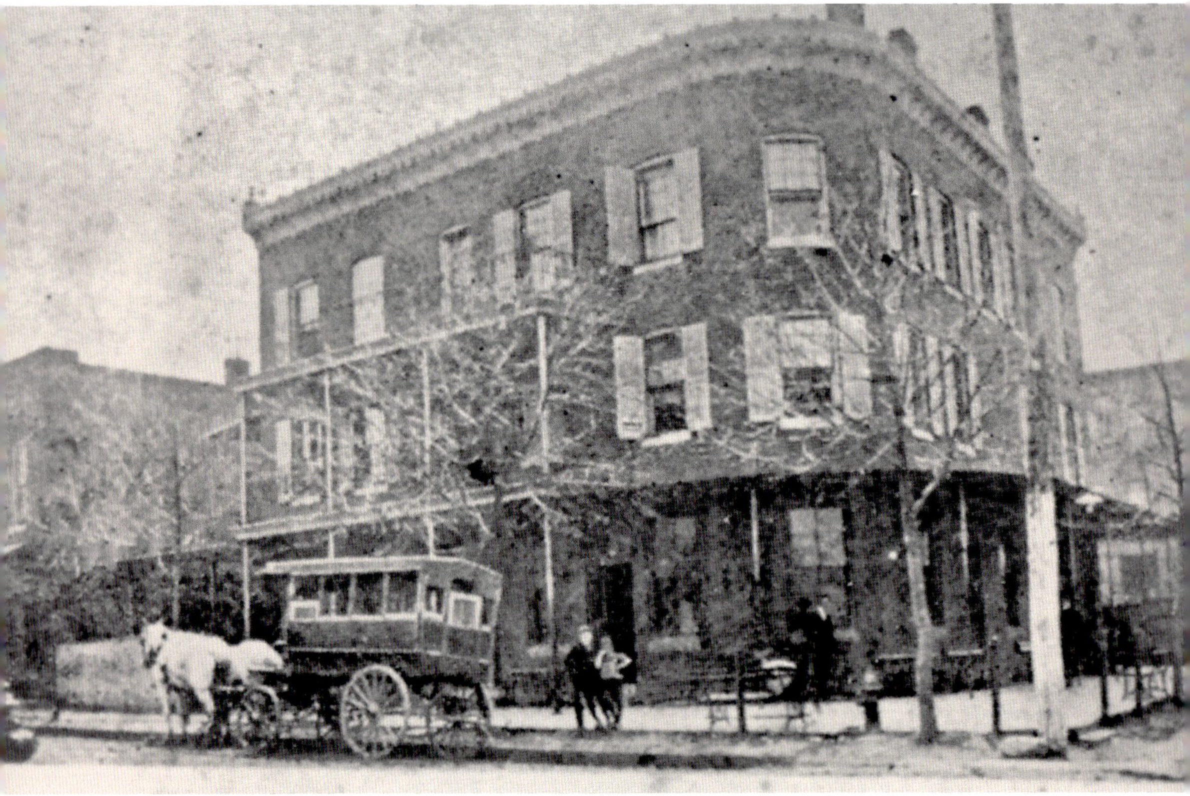

The Hotel Purnell was located on the corner of Green and North Washington Streets and was the rest stop for visitors heading to Public Landing. The building is said to have had marble floors, a wonderful restaurant, and more-than-comfortable accommodations. The building was torn down. The new building in its place was once home to Edgehill Pharmacy and is now occupied by the Tri-County Council. (Then photograph courtesy of Worcester County Library; now photograph by the author.)

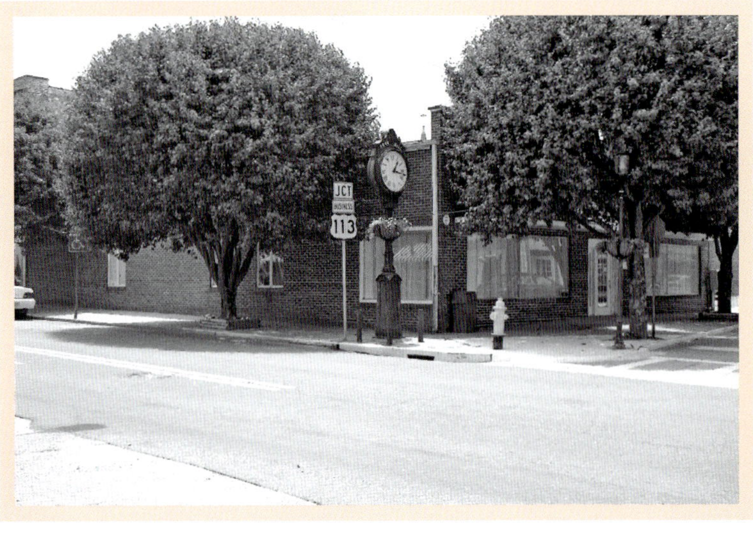

CHAPTER 3

CIVIL SERVICE

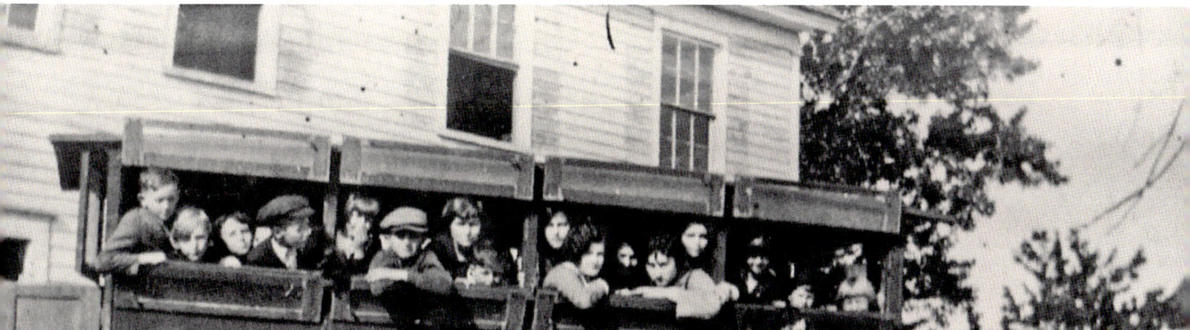

Harvey Pusey owned and drove the first bus in Worcester County. His bus is pictured here with a female bus driver. The identities of the 16 students and the bus driver are unknown. The bus driver is said to be Pusey's wife, but this is not confirmed. The year is also unconfirmed. (Courtesy of the Purnell Museum.)

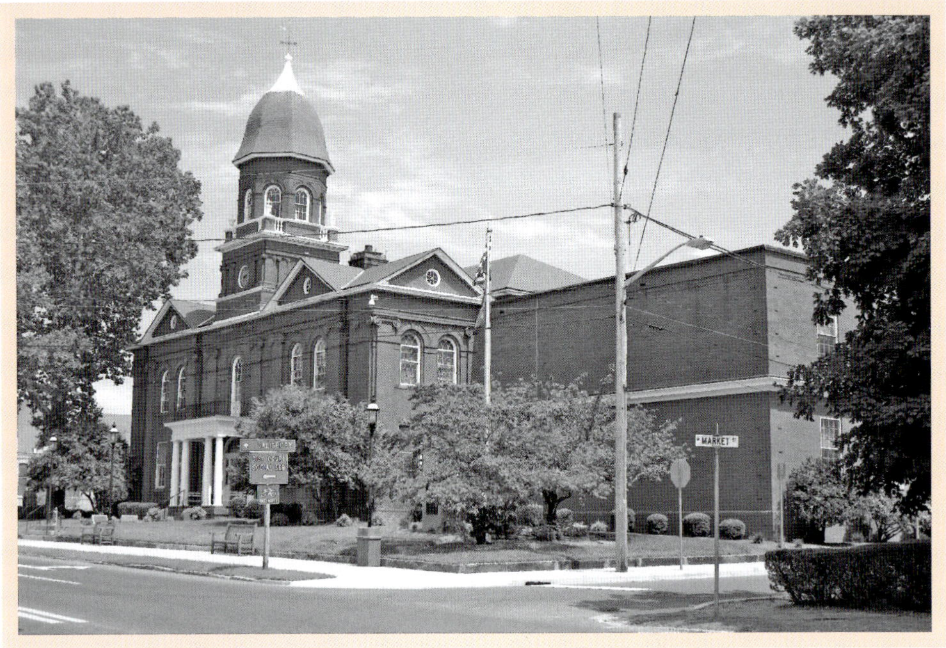

This building is the Worcester County Courthouse. The original two courthouses burned, and this building was constructed in their place in 1894. The land it sits on was the original land of the other destroyed courthouses also. Now about 200 people are employed in this building, including Worcester County 911, environmental services, the circuit court, the sheriff's office, the treasurer's office and much more. (Then photograph courtesy of Worcester County Library; now photograph by the author.)

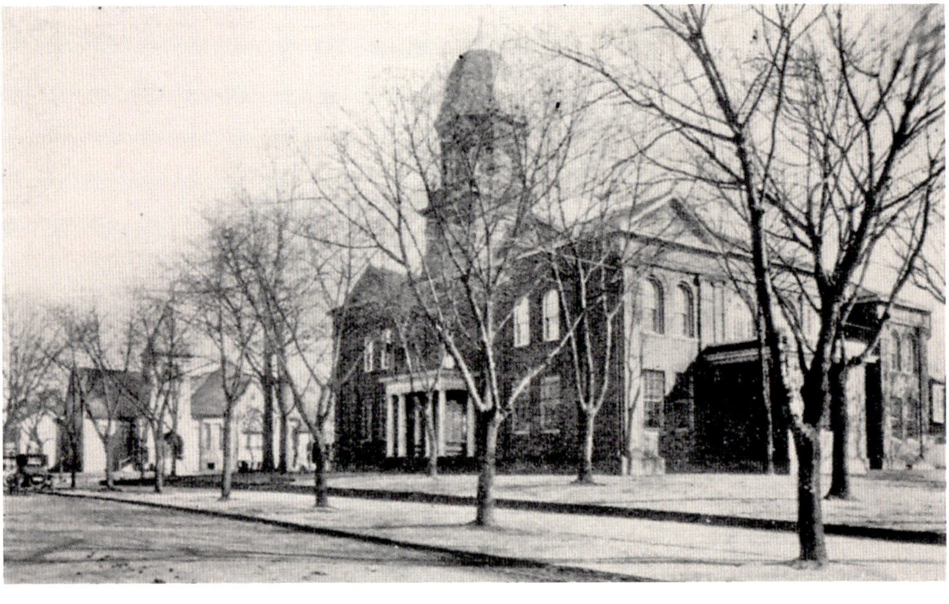

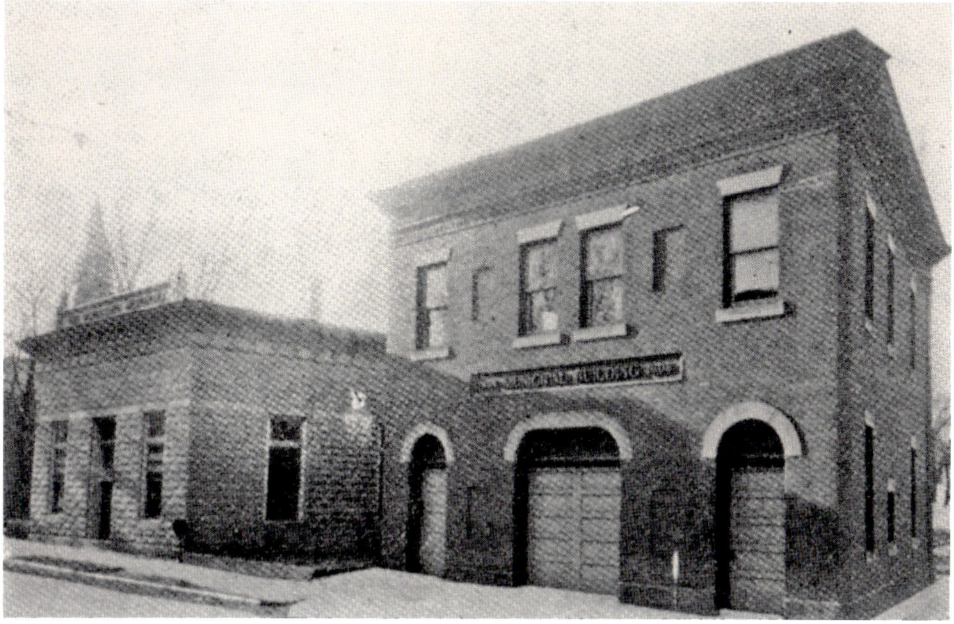

The Municipal Building was constructed in 1908 and was once home to the mayor's office and the Snow Hill Volunteer Fire Department. Later the fire department was relocated. The mayor's offices still remains but is operated as town hall. (Then photograph courtesy of Worcester County Library; now photograph by the author.)

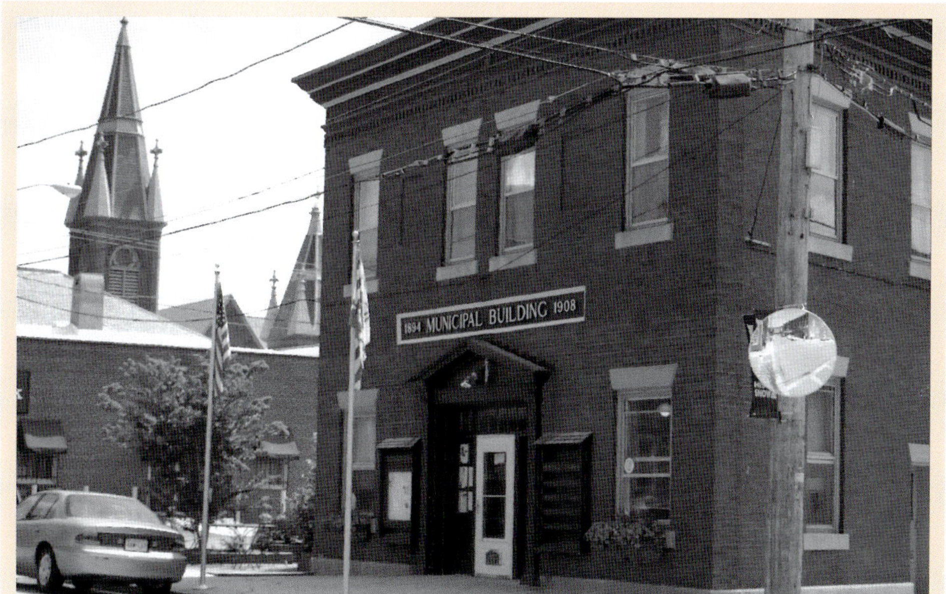

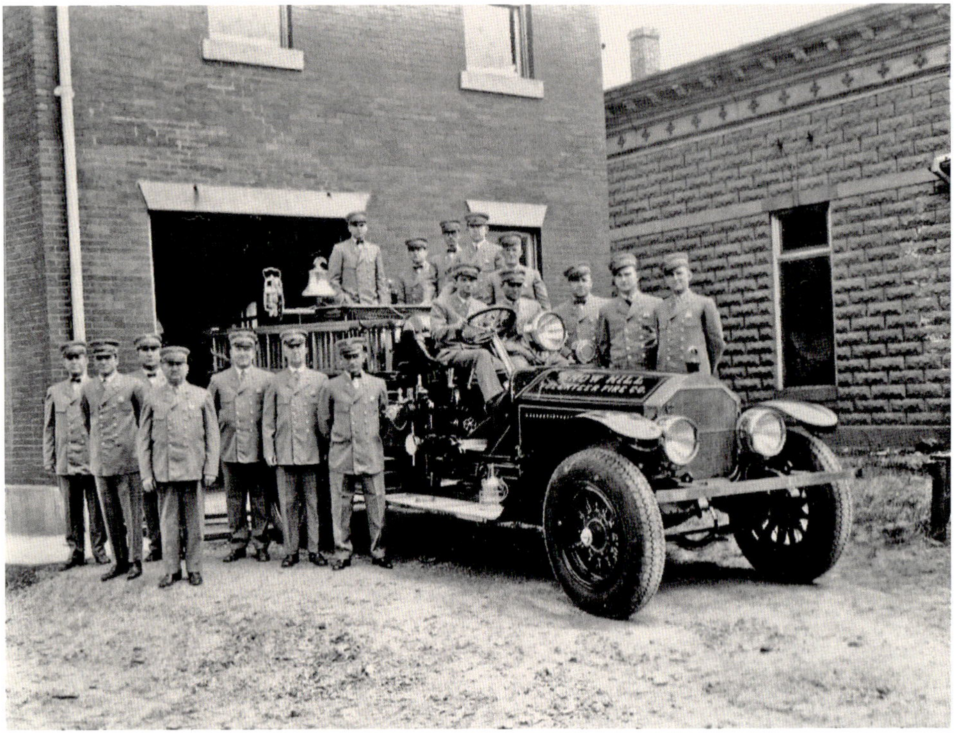

The Snow Hill Volunteer Fire Department was originally located in the Municipal Building, along with the mayor's office, on West Green and Bank Streets. The fire department moved across the street and eventually had a new department built on the south end of Church Street. Now the fire truck doors have been bricked in, and the nearly attached building has a little sitting area and parking in its place. Below is a rear view of town hall. (Then photograph courtesy of the Worcester County Library; now photograph by the author.)

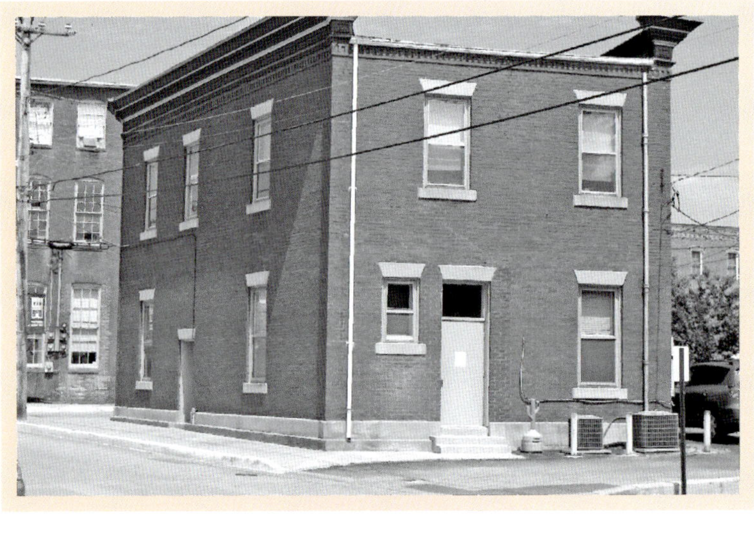

CHAPTER 4

Historic Homes and Byways

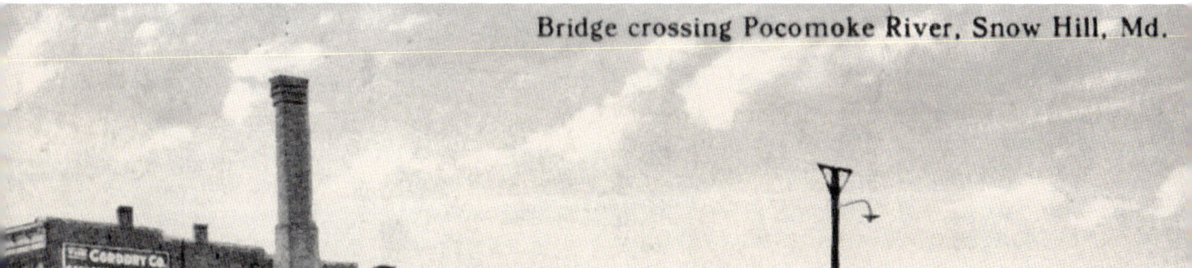

The Pocomoke River Bridge was erected in 1932; it is the smallest moving bridge in Maryland and one of the oldest. Route 12 passes over the Pocomoke River to Snow Hill's North Washington Street. Today the original bridge keeper's house is intact and is still used to raise and lower the bridge for boaters. (Then photograph courtesy of Worcester County Library.)

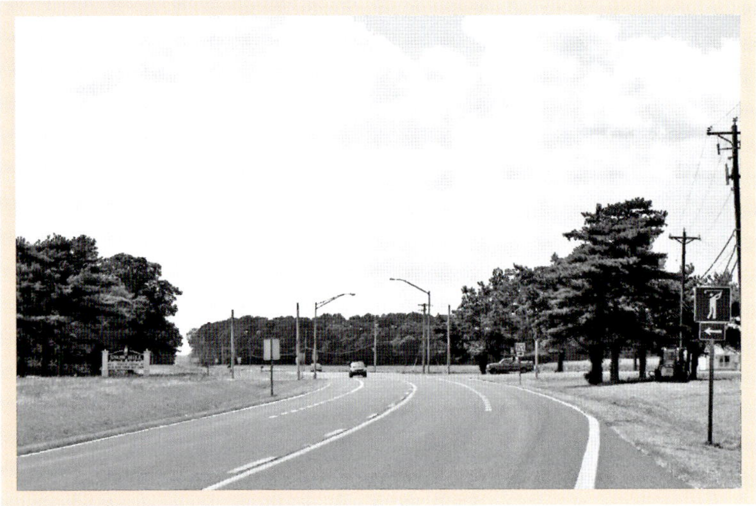

The old causeway road, also known as the Indian trail, is pictured below as a dirt road. The trail was used to bring goods such as lumber, food, and crafts into Snow Hill. People would travel from Indiantown and Furnace Town on the old causeway road into Snow Hill for the day. Today this stretch of road, known as Route 12, joins Salisbury and Snow Hill. Many people still travel from Salisbury to Snow Hill for work today. (Then photograph courtesy of Worcester County Library; now photograph by the author.)

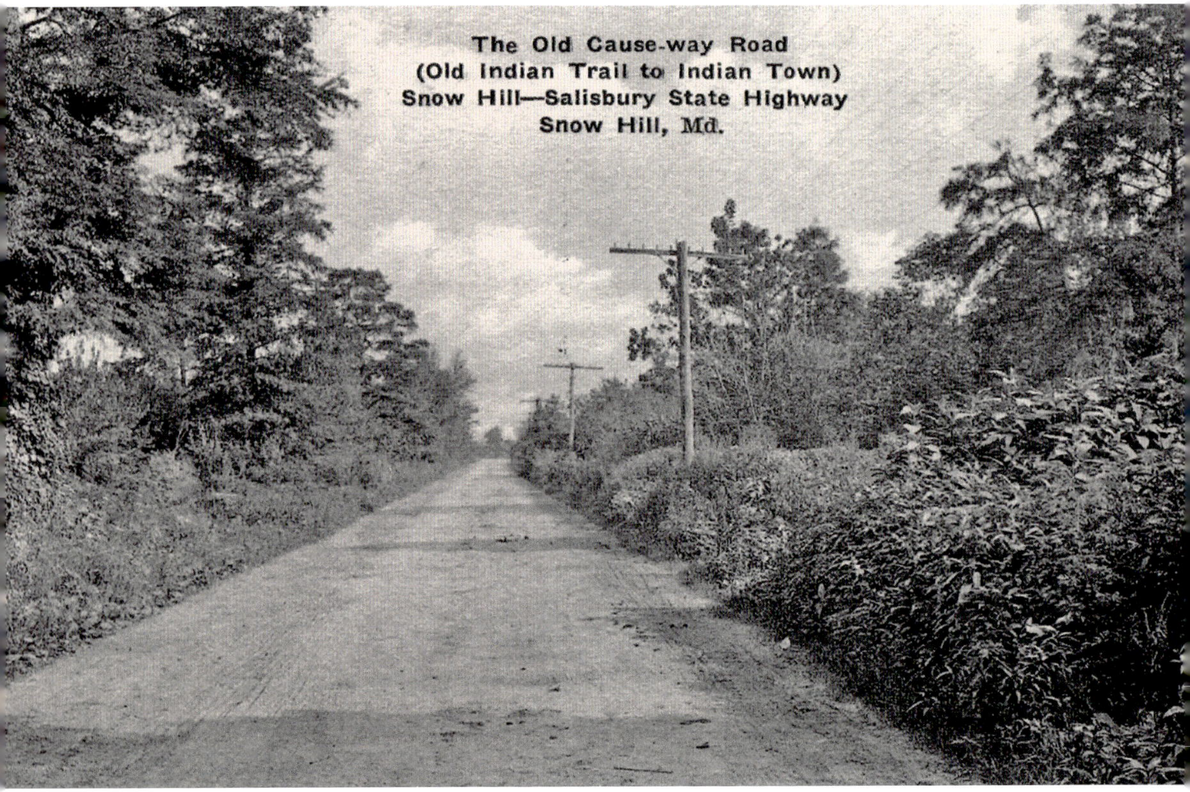

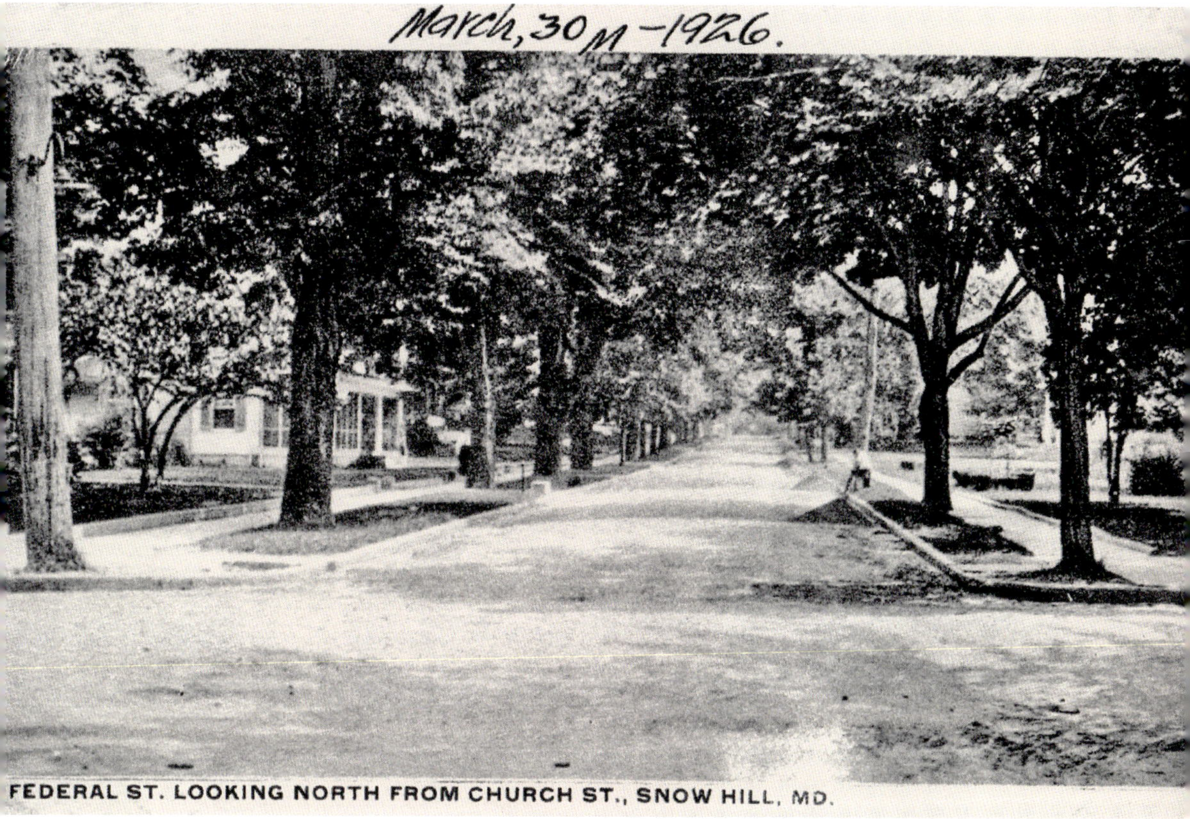

Above, Federal Street looking north from Church Street in March 1926 shows concrete sidewalks, planted trees, and utility poles. Today not much has changed, and aside from growth, the houses remain the same also. Federal Street and Church Street is where the majority of the first homes were built in Snow Hill. (Then photograph courtesy of Worcester County Library; now photograph by the author.)

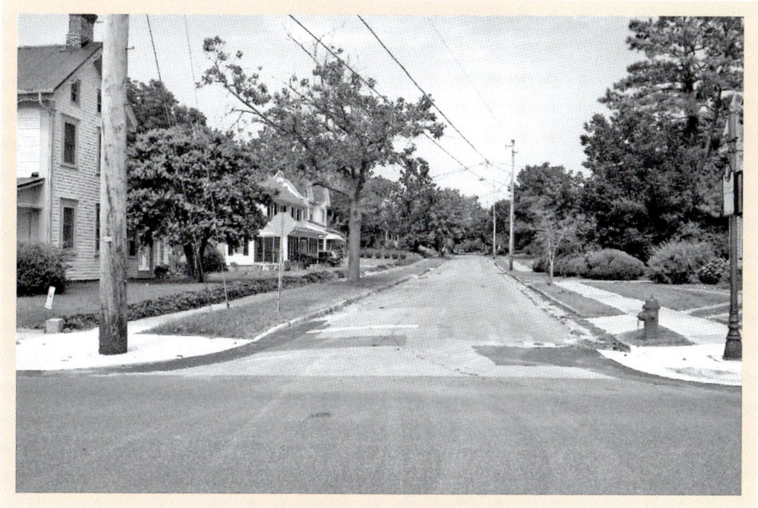

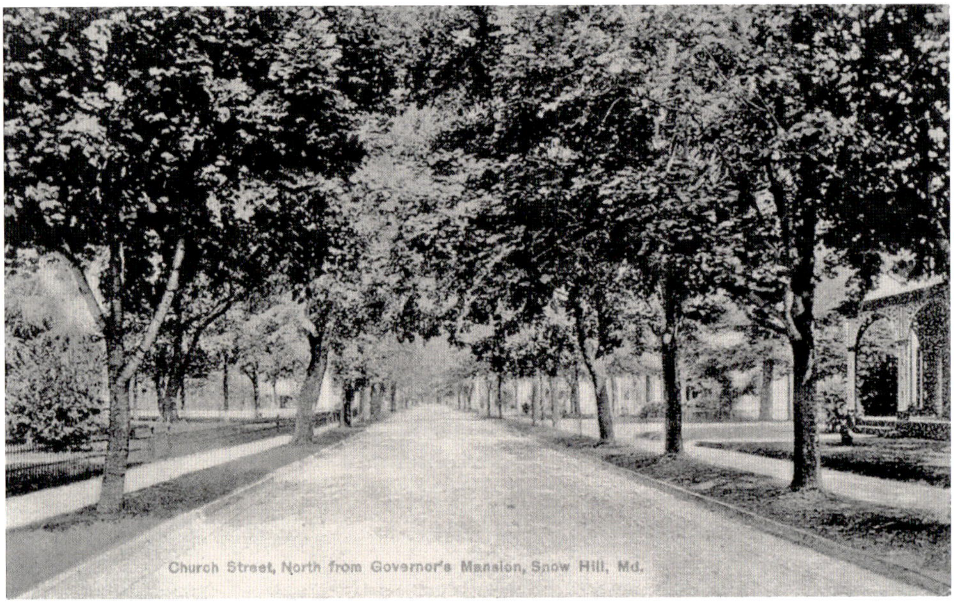

Church Street looking north from the governor's mansion is pictured above, with trees neatly lining the sidewalks. Today some of the same trees remain, and this street is also Route 12, which runs from Salisbury south through Snow Hill, Girdle Tree, and Stockton into Virginia. Snow Hill High School and the Snow Hill Fire Department also call Church Street home. (Then photograph courtesy of Worcester County Library; now photograph by the author.)

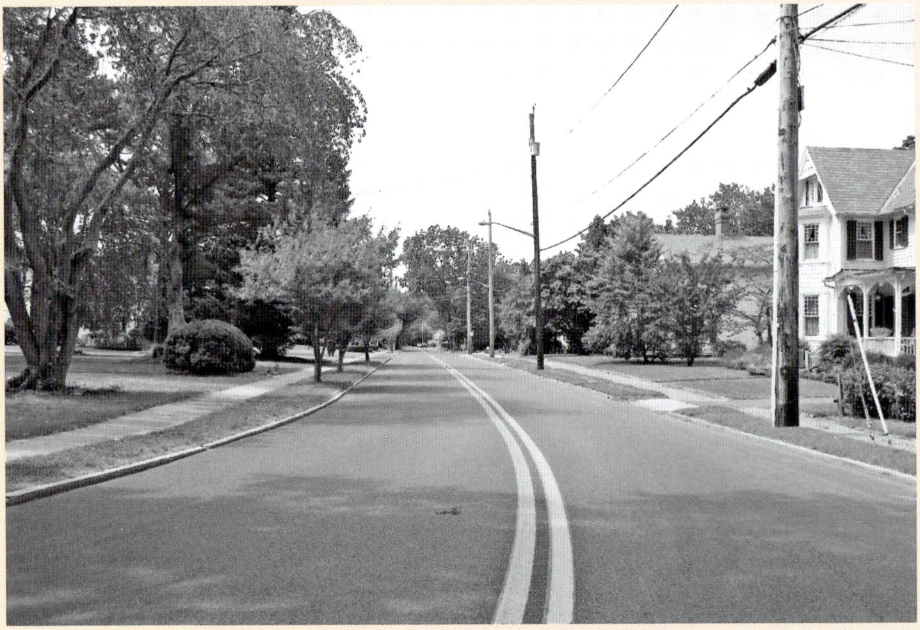

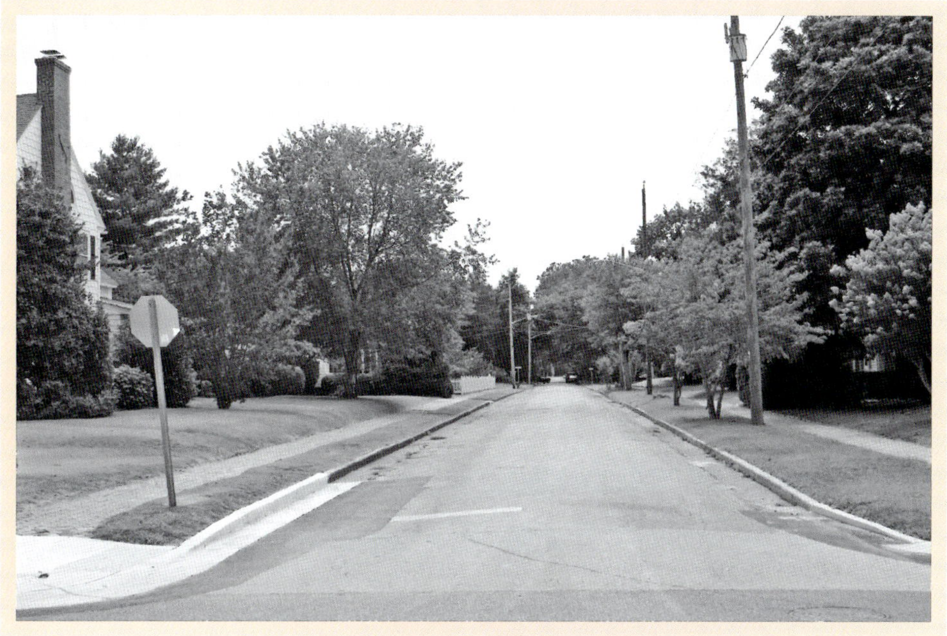

Federal Street looking west from Church Street is pictured below with fencing on its left side surrounding the homes up to Division Street. The fence no longer exists, but the owners of the last home before Division Street have since put up a fence to enclose the yard. The homes pictured are still standing, with minor renovations. (Then photograph courtesy of Worcester County Library; now photograph by the author.)

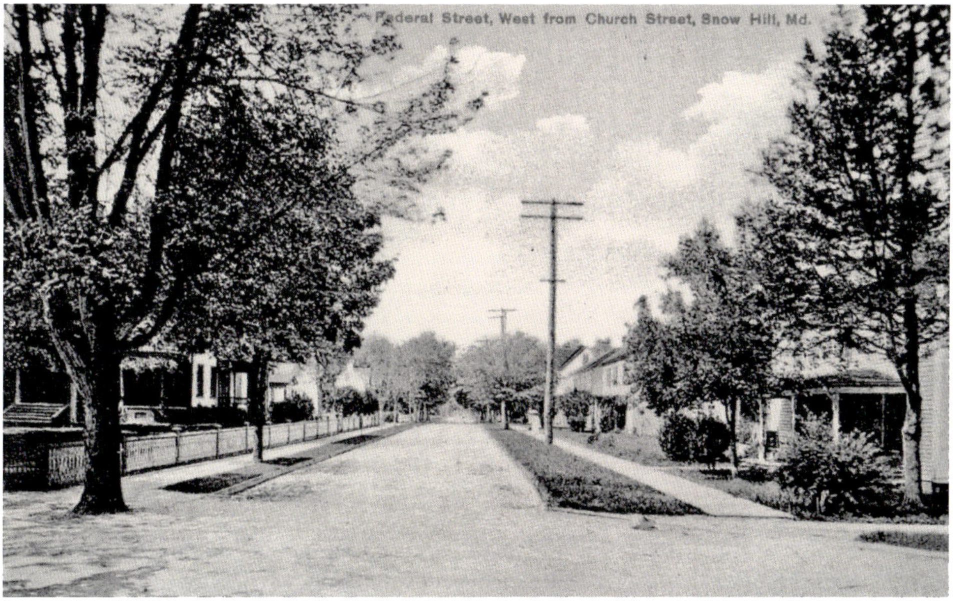

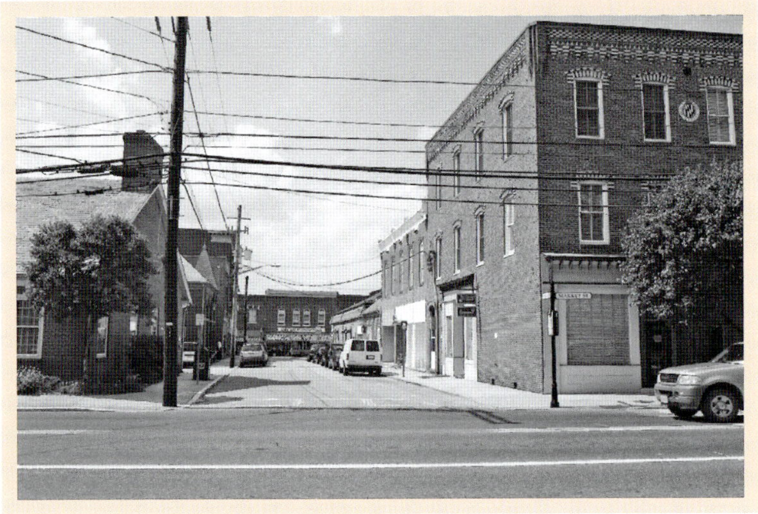

Pearl Street is pictured below from the courthouse. The *Democratic Messenger* building is directly across from the courthouse. The Messenger building was constructed between 1893 and 1894 and was one of the first buildings built after the fire of 1893. Opposite the Messenger building is the bank. The *Democratic Messenger* is no longer in print, and the building is occupied by the county tourism office. Taylor Bank now operates on the other corner. The entrance of the bank has been moved, and a drive-through has been added. Barry Laws of Snow Hill is the bank manager. (Then photograph courtesy of Worcester County Library; now photograph by the author.)

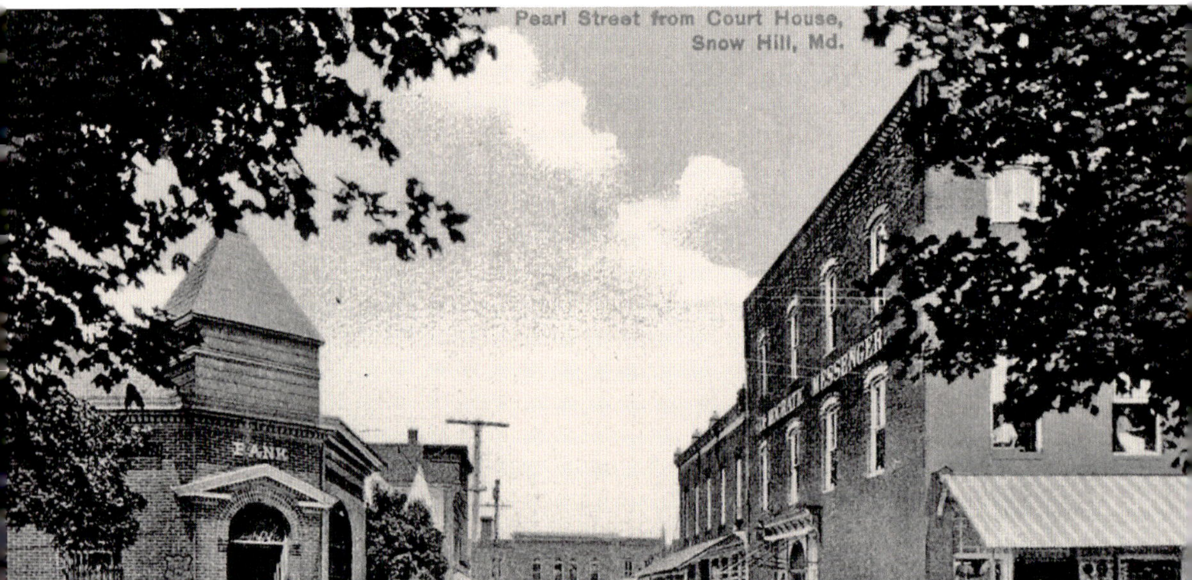

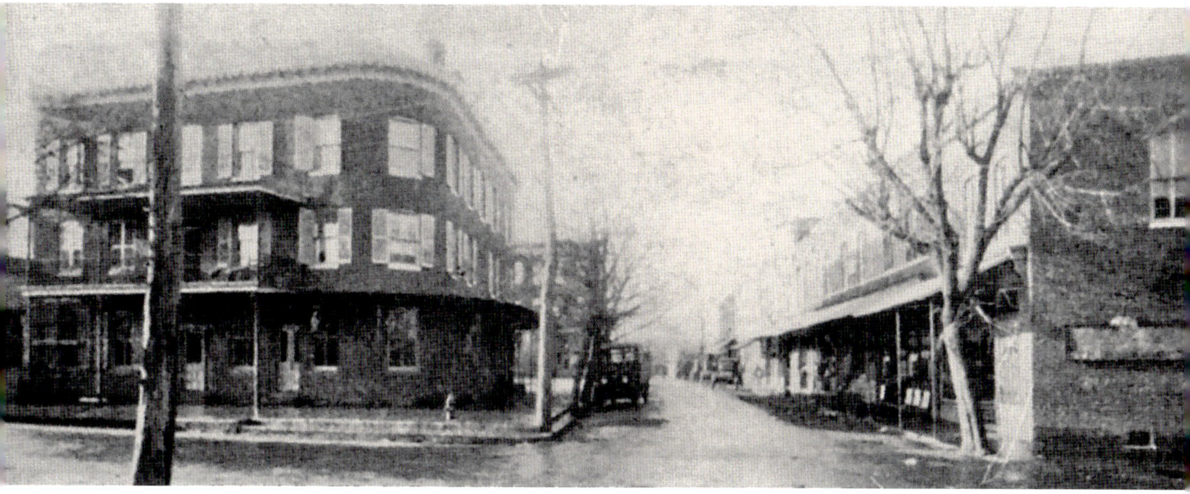

The Purnell Hotel was on the corner of West Green and North Washington Streets. The building, dating back to 1894, occupied the land Washington Tavern was on before the 1893 fire. Green Street was lined with merchants, including a mattress shop, a pharmacy, and a butcher. Now Green Street prospers with Snow Hill Flowers and Gifts, owned by Nikki Elliot and her mother, Barbara Taylor; the Palette, a contemporary restaurant owned by Raye Whaley; Lost in the Country; and the American Legion. The Purnell Hotel no longer exists; a one-story building was put in its place in the mid-1960s. That building was home to Edgehill Pharmacy and now is the office of the Tri-County Council. (Then photograph courtesy of Worcester County Library; now photograph by the author.)

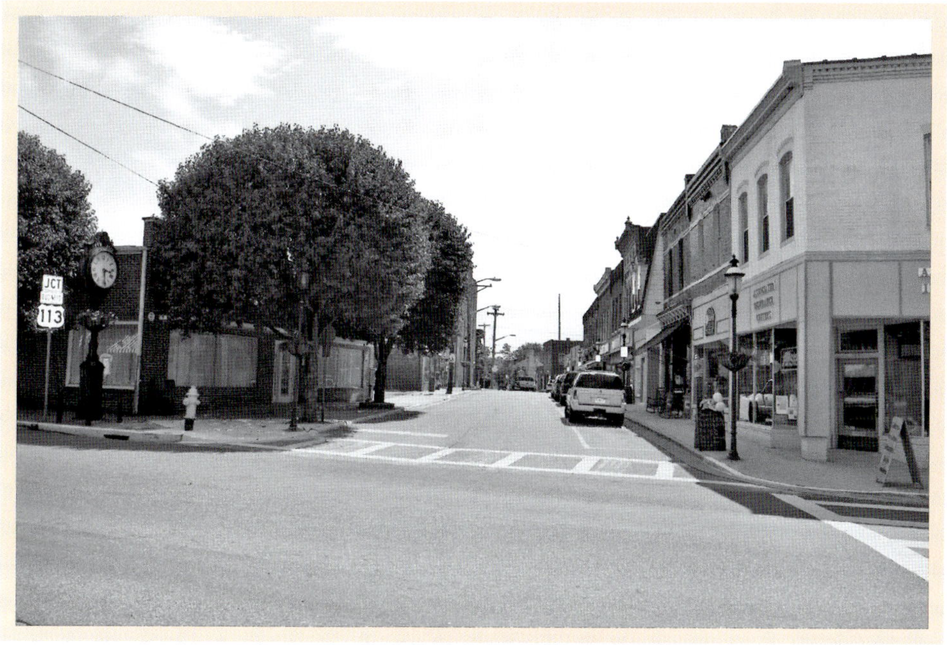

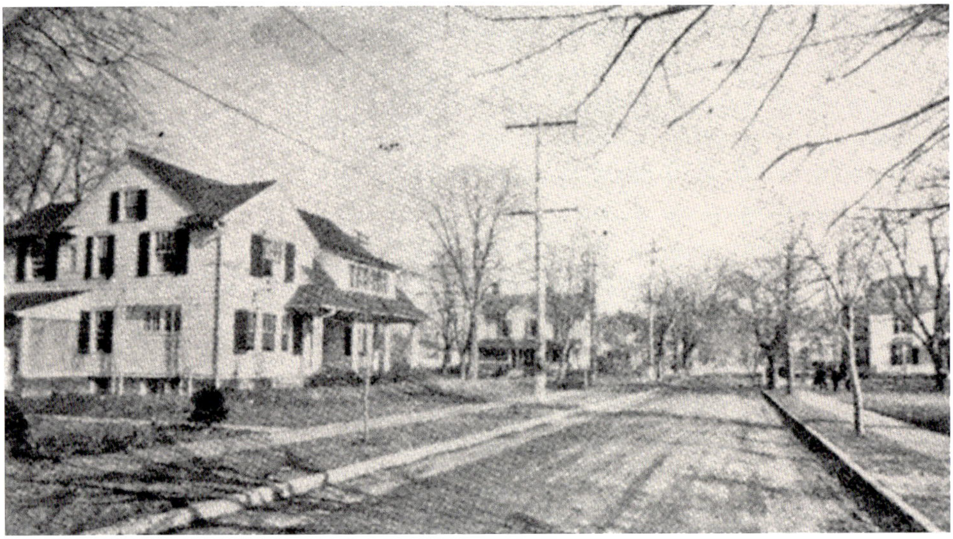

The above picture, captured in the early 1900s, shows the corner of Federal Street facing Church Street. All of these homes remain amid the growth. In the far right is the *c.* 1887 Hargis Shockley house, in the far left sits the *c.* 1873 P. D. Cottingham house, and the house in the forefront is unknown. A fence lined the right side of Federal Street but has since been removed. (Then photograph courtesy of Worcester County Library; now photograph by the author.)

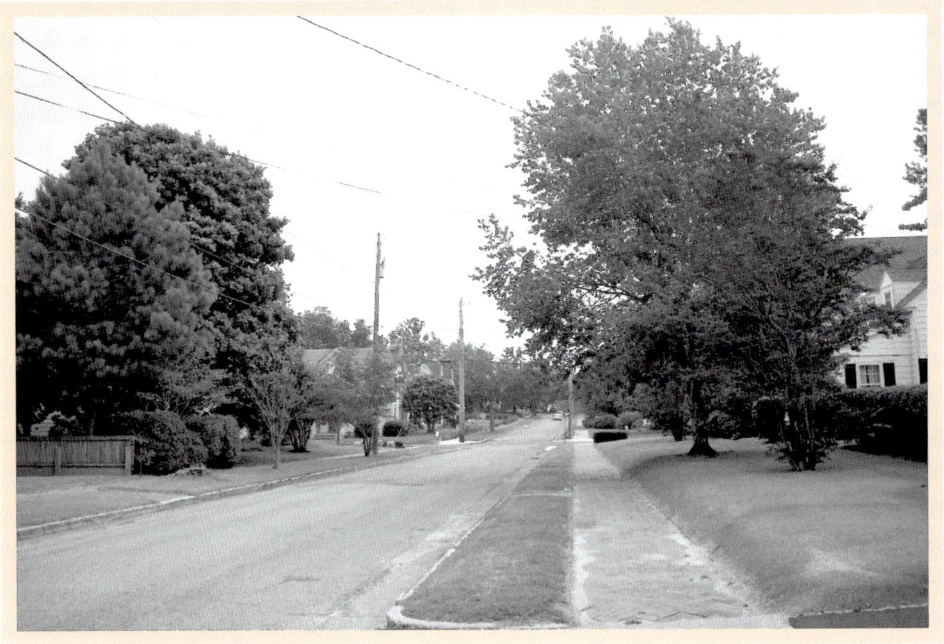

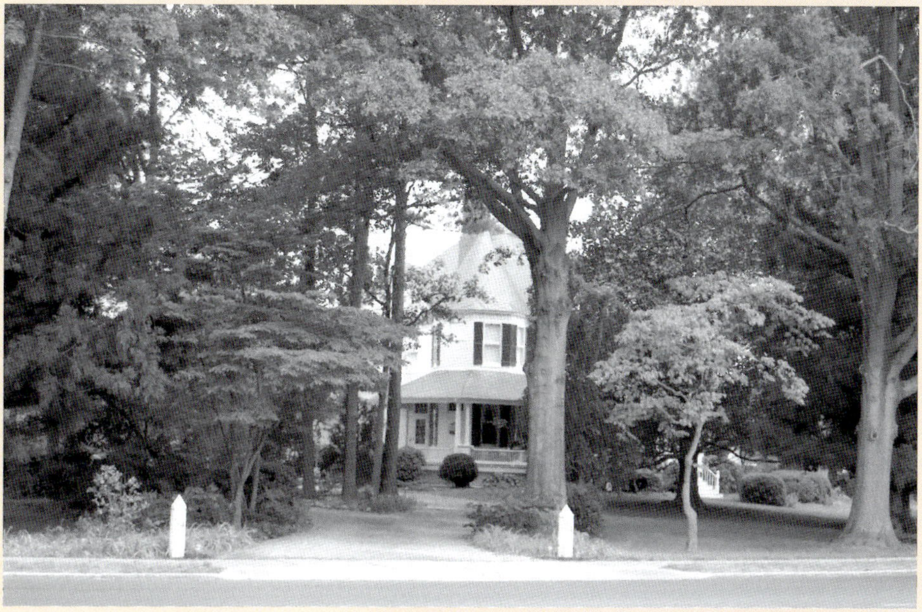

The photograph below is an early-1900s picture of the corner of Church Street. The governor's mansion is hidden in the trees, and this property was once lined with a small knee fence. Today the house is still erect, but the fence has been removed. Church Street is still one of the town's most traveled roads. (Then photograph courtesy of Worcester County Library; now photograph by the author.)

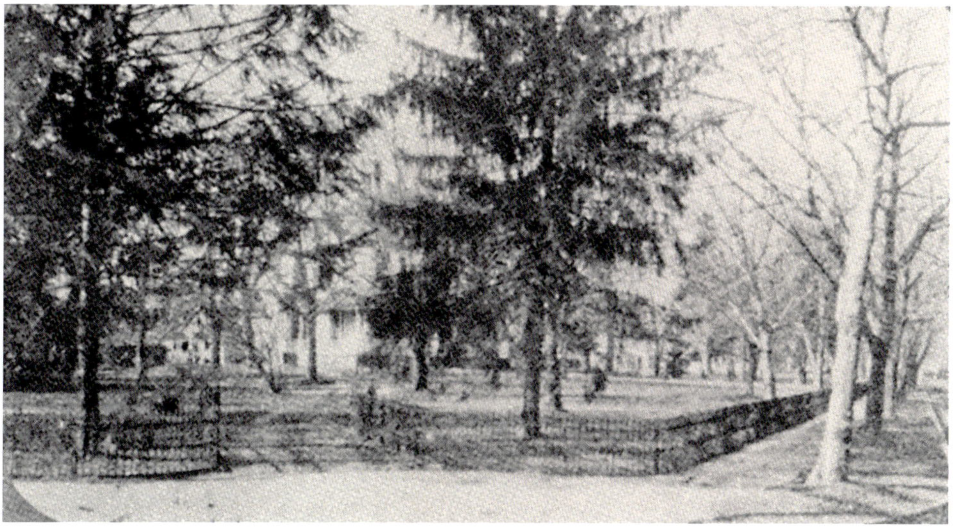

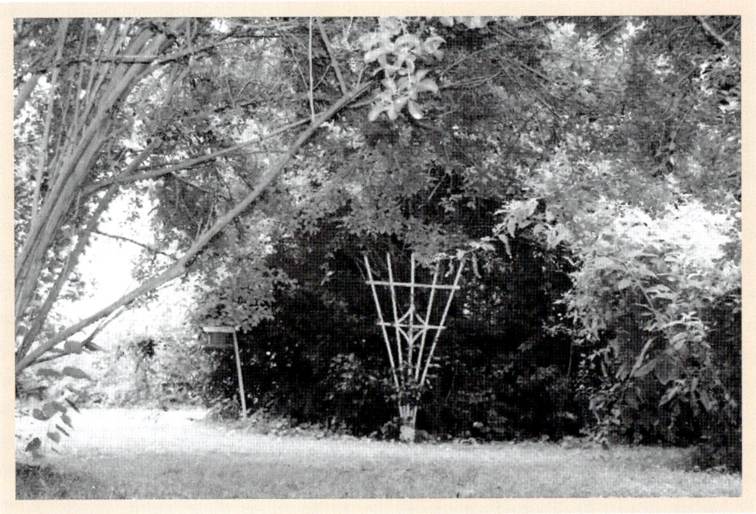

The undated scene below is said to be the gardens around the George S. Payne house on the corner of West Federal and Morris Streets. Today, though the gardens have grown up, the George S. Payne house still has some beautiful views from the street. (Then photograph courtesy of Worcester County Library; now photograph by the author.)

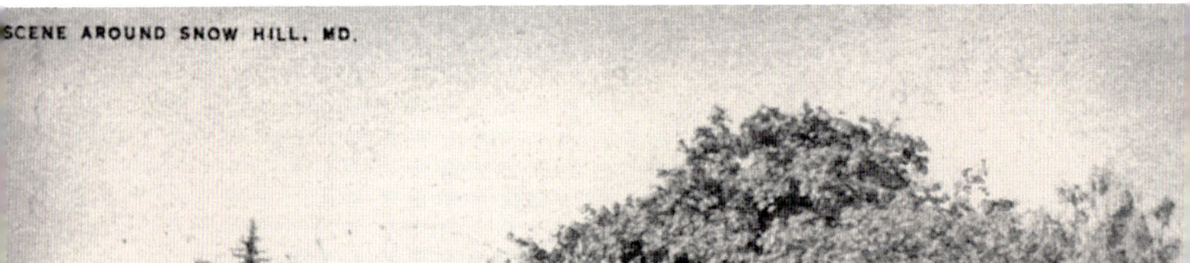

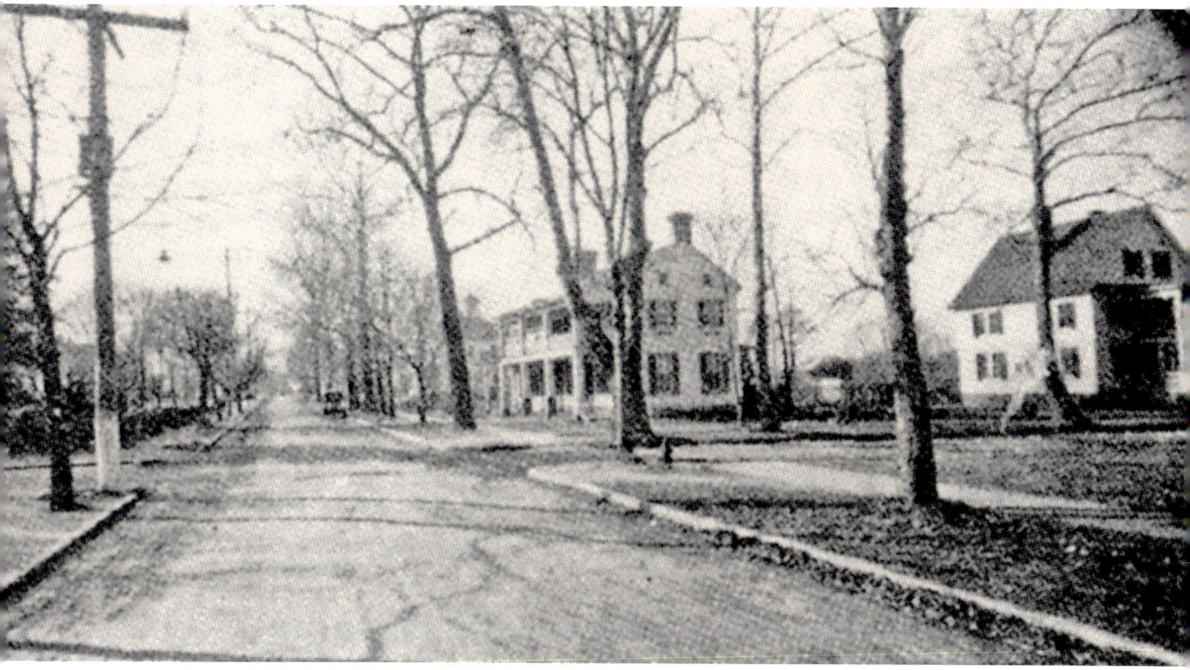

Looking up Federal Street to Morris Street, one can see the William H. Farrow house on the corner. Construction began around 1810, with additions in 1825 and 1850. The house farthest right is unknown. This home is directly across the street from the George S. Payne house on the corner of West Federal Street. Today the gardens around the house have been well maintained, as has the original structure. (Then photograph courtesy of Worcester County Library; now photograph by the author.)

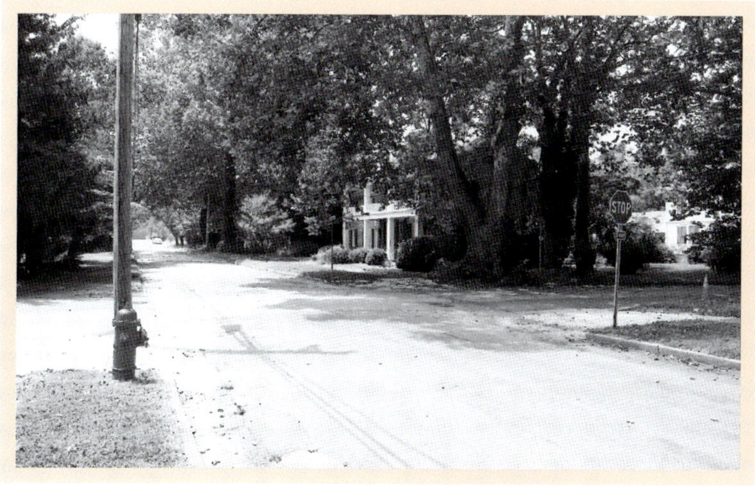

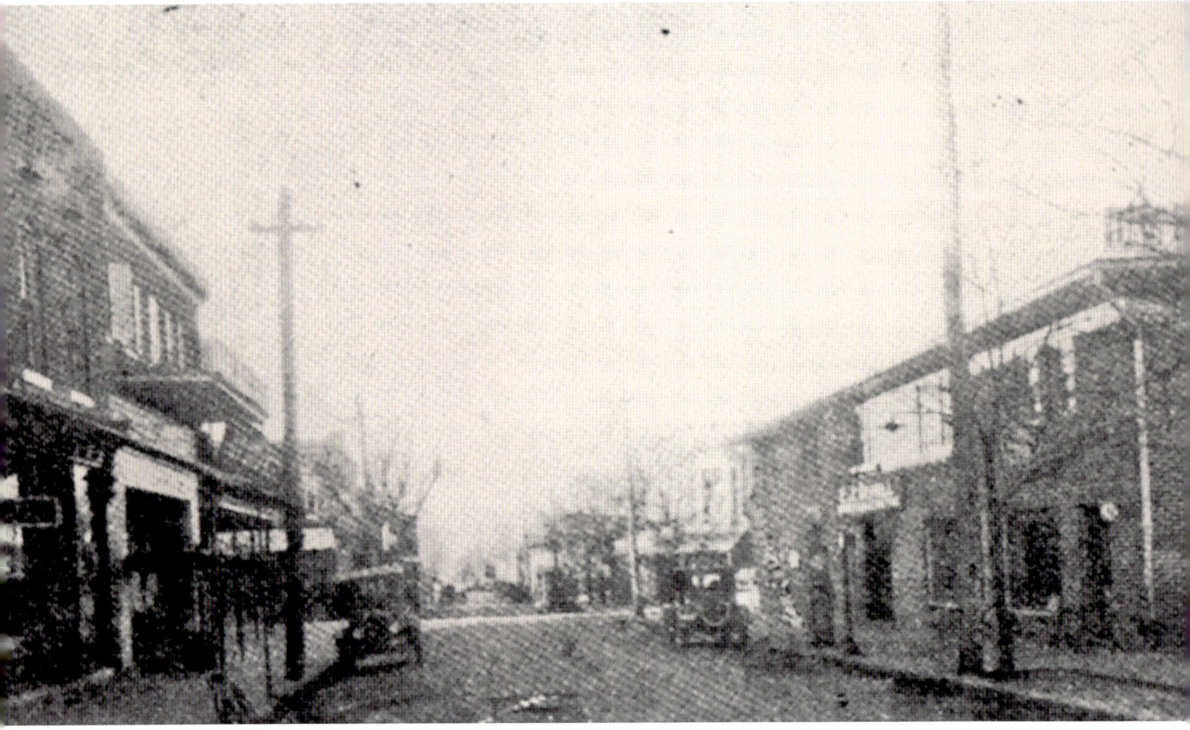

In the late 1800s and early 1900s, business in Snow Hill was booming. Green Street had many merchants. Pictured above is Green Street looking toward Washington Street at an unknown date. Today Green Street still has the same look and is still lined with filled storefronts. (Then photograph courtesy of Worcester County Library; now photograph by the author.)

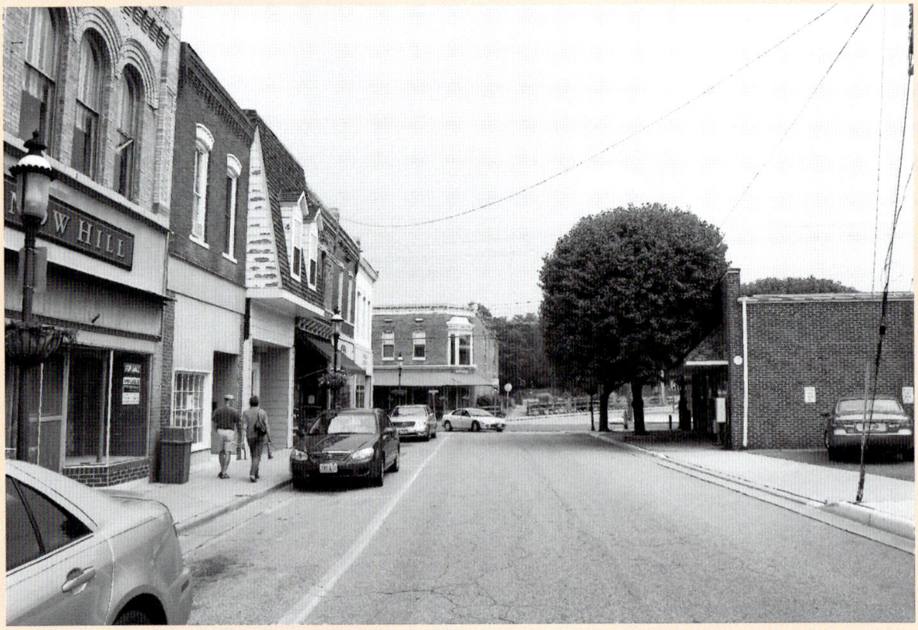

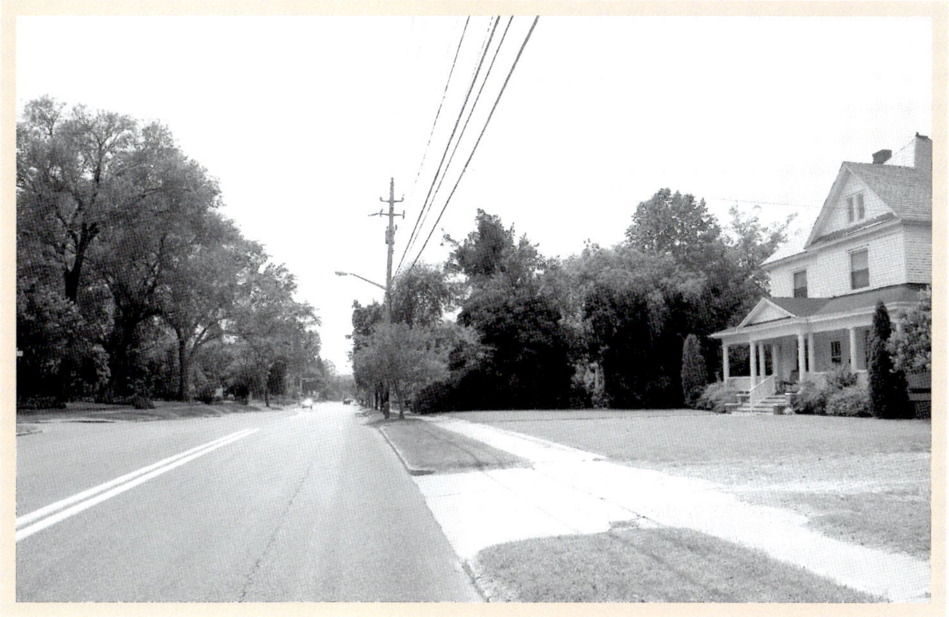

Pearl Street is pictured below from the courthouse in this undated postcard. The *Democratic Messenger* building is on the right corner, and there is a bank on the left. The *Democratic Messenger* newspaper was in business some 20 years. Today Taylor Bank, run by Barry Laws, is on the left corner of Pearl Street, and the tourism offices for Worcester County occupy the Messenger building. (Then photograph courtesy of Worcester County Library; now photograph by the author.)

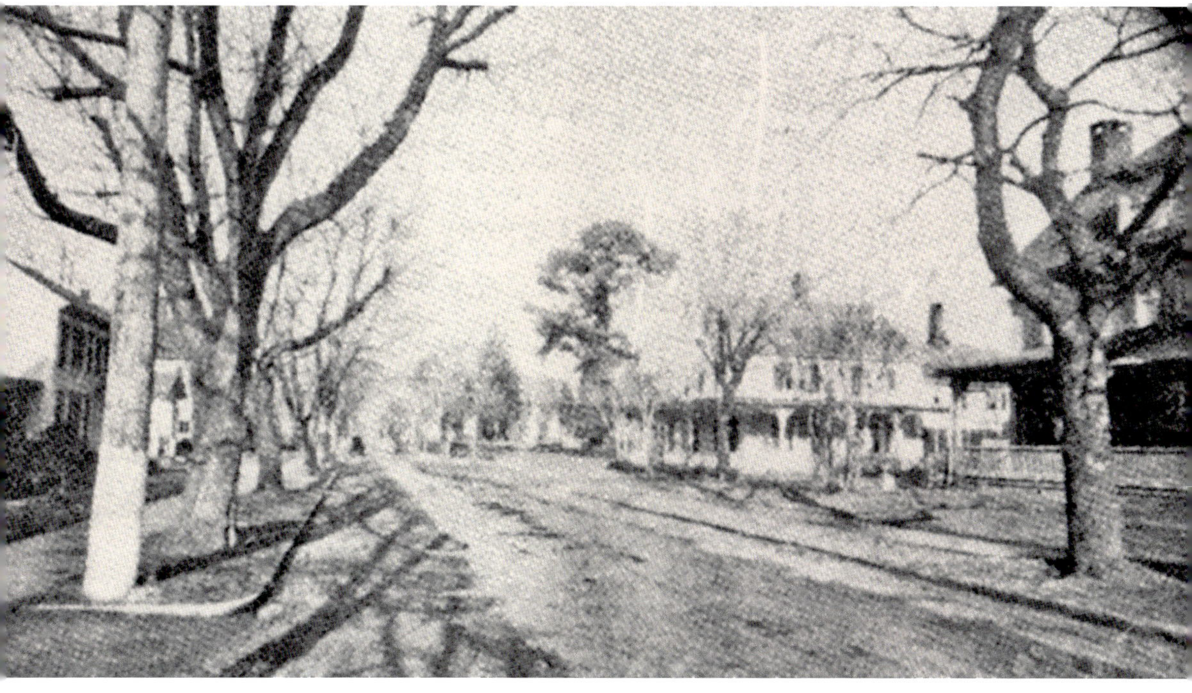

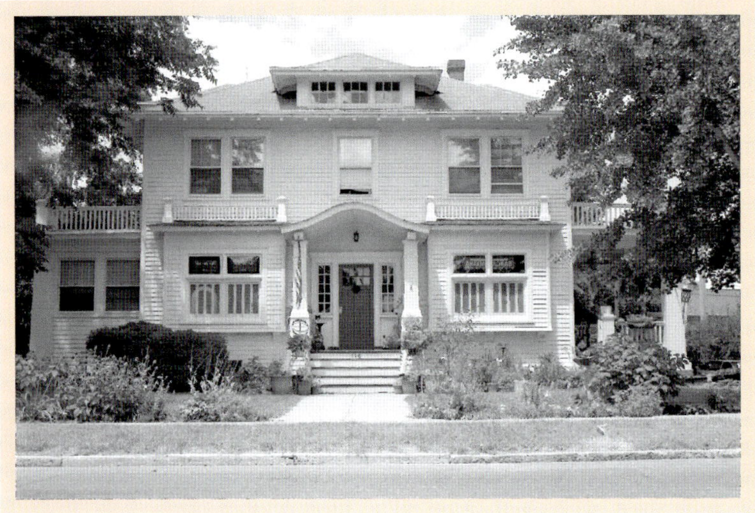

Not unlike many of the homes in Snow Hill, the Charles W. Corddry house was built in the early 20th century. This bungalow-style home's construction was financed by then-mayor Charles Corddry in 1924. Charles was son to William S Corddry Sr., who founded W. D. Corddry Lumber Company. Today the home is owned by Fran and Bill Price. (Then photograph courtesy of Worcester County Library; now photograph by the author.)

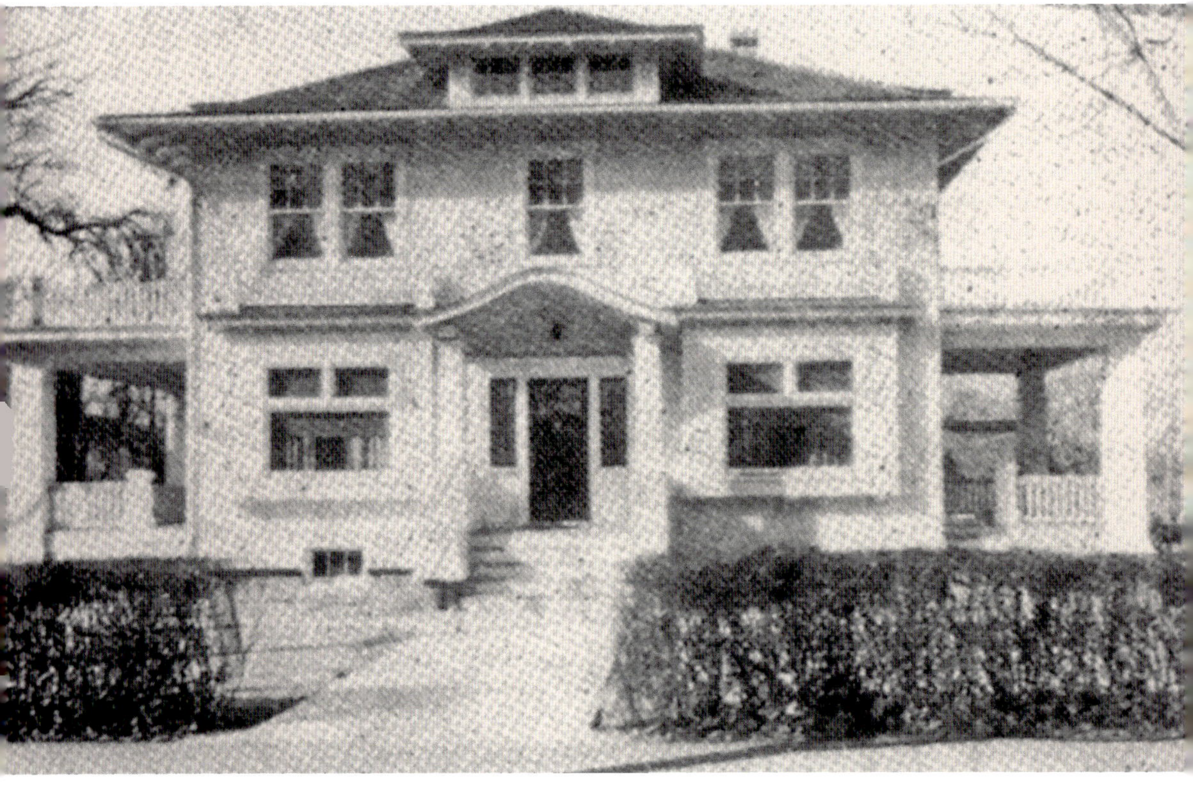

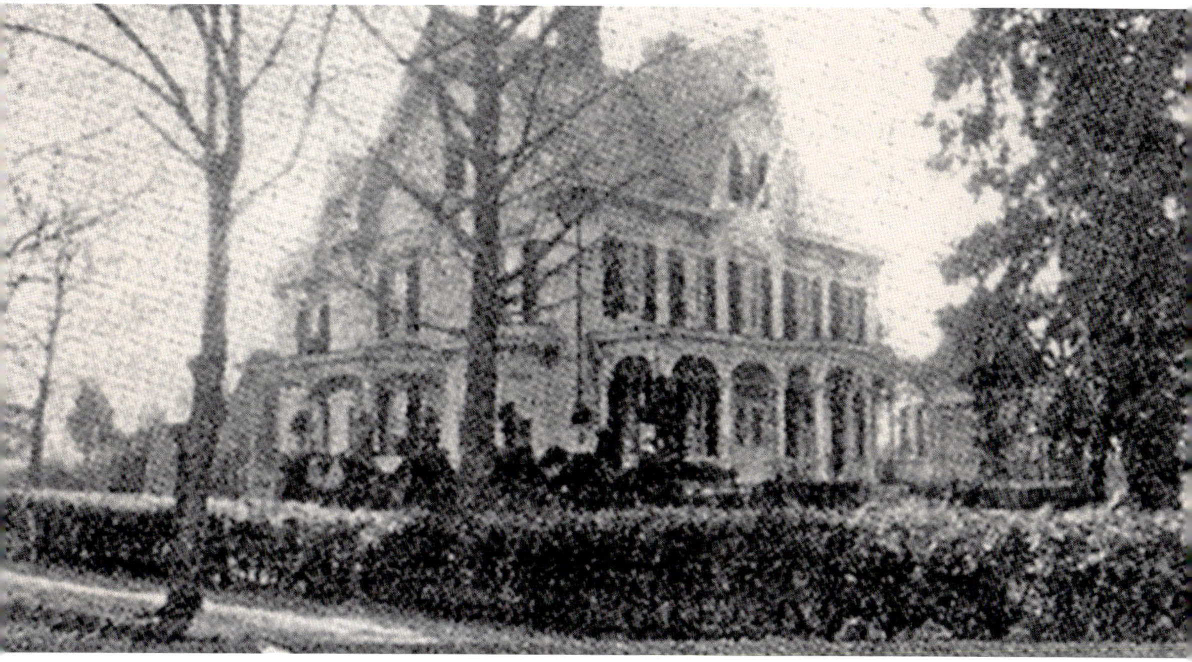

Originally owned by George S. Payne, Mapleton is located on the corner of Morris and West Federal Streets. The Victorian domestic architecture of this home is similar to Gothic Revival architecture. The front and end gables of this home are covered in fish-scale shingles, and the original porch is intact. G. S. Payne financed the construction of this home in 1881 but did not own it until 1883. He died in 1926, and the home passed down to Winifred M. and Nellie M. Payne. Now it is enclosed by growth. The Pusey family of Snow Hill currently owns the home. (Then photograph courtesy of Worcester County Library; now photograph by the author.)

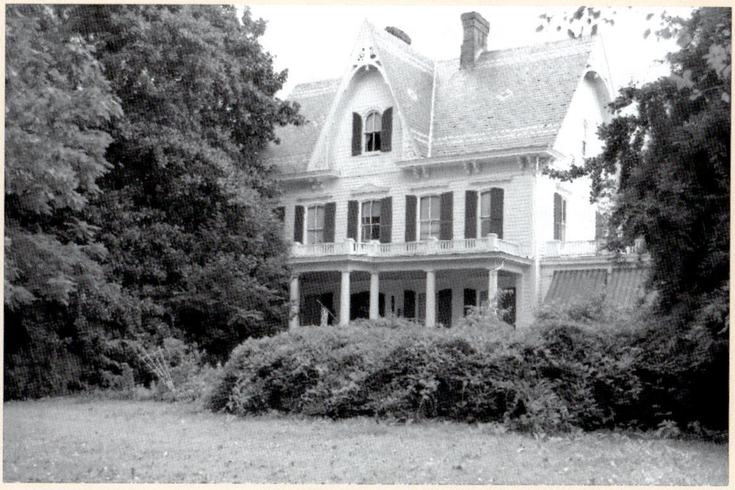

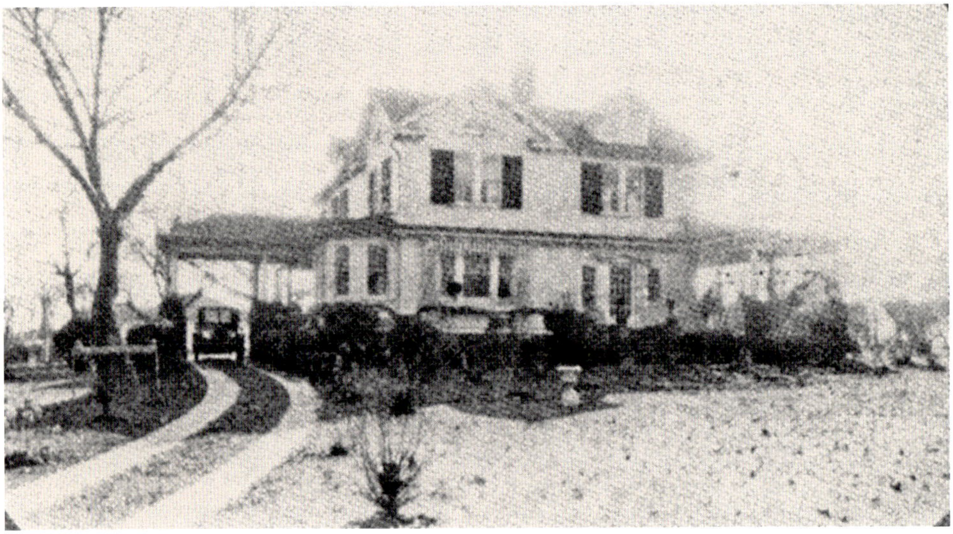

The Frank Fooks home on the west end of Federal Street is a neighbor to Mapleton. Frank Fooks built this home and lived in it until his death in 1933. His daughter Sarah, born in 1928, lived in the home until 2002, and Ron and Hazel Geesey bought and remodeled the entire property. The home is now surrounded with beautiful flower, vegetable, and herb gardens. There have since been additions onto the home, and an in-ground saltwater pool has been added and landscaped. (Then photograph courtesy of Worcester County Library; now photograph by the author.)

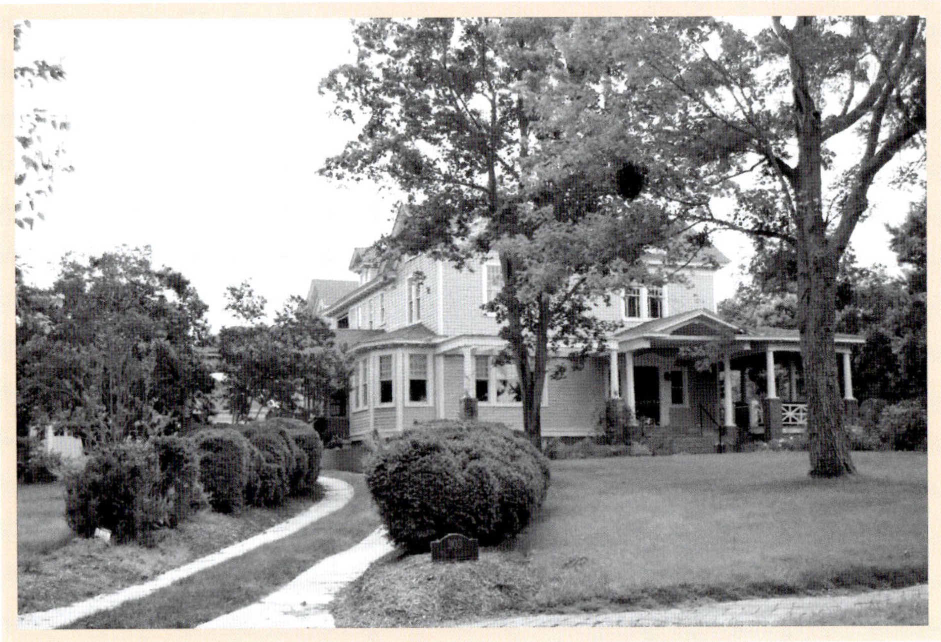

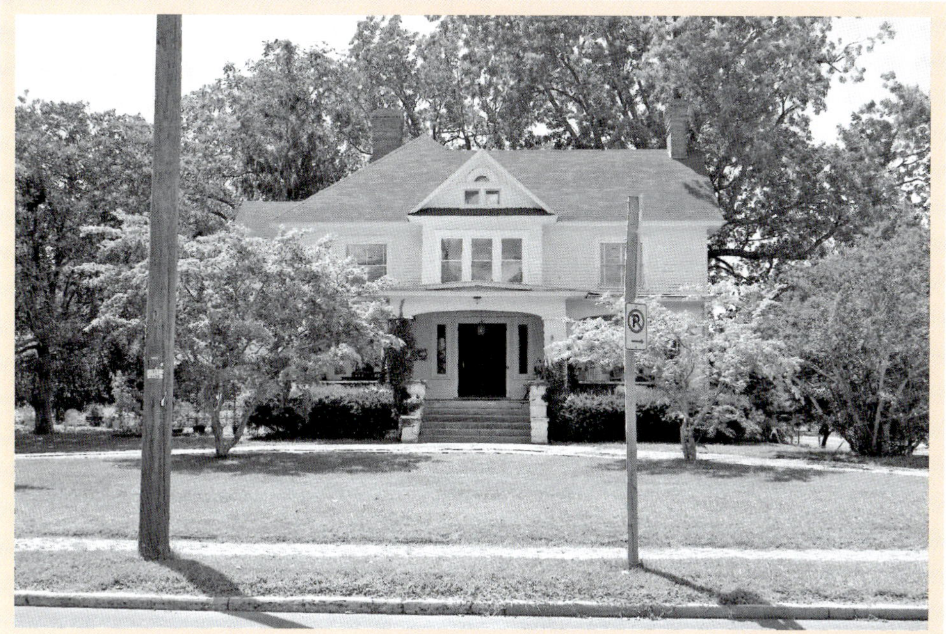

The 1905 L-shaped Purnell-Shockley house sits on the south corner of Church and Market Streets. The first record of improvements was not until 1965. Samuel H. Jarman and Littleton R. Purnell were the deed holders at that time. The Purnell ownership of the home was not over until 1940. In 1941, Walter and Addie Shockley bought the home. Addie kept the house a few years after her husband's death, but in 1978, she sold it. The home has had great upkeep and is one of the largest in Snow Hill. (Then photograph courtesy of Worcester County Library; now photograph by the author.)

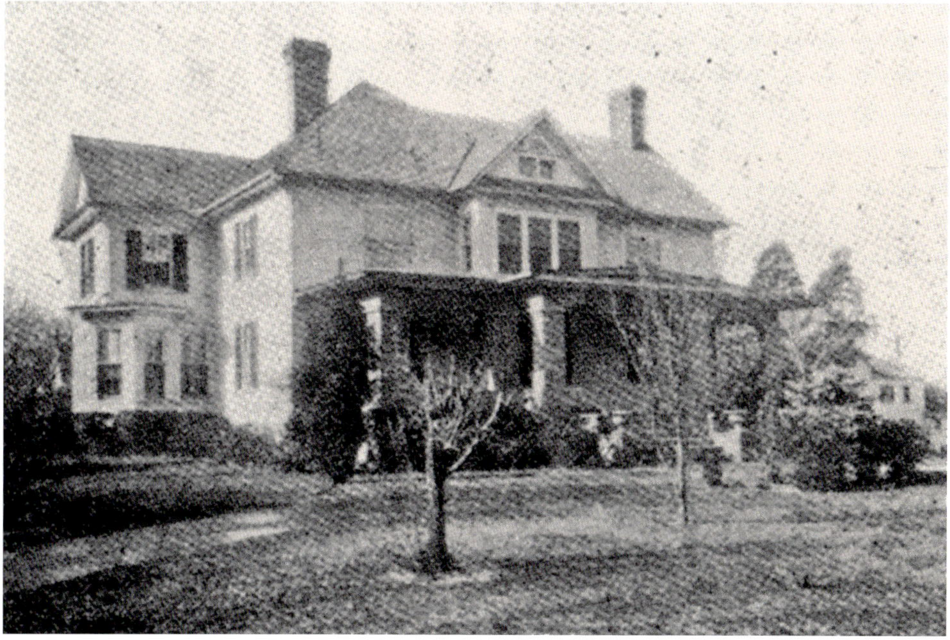

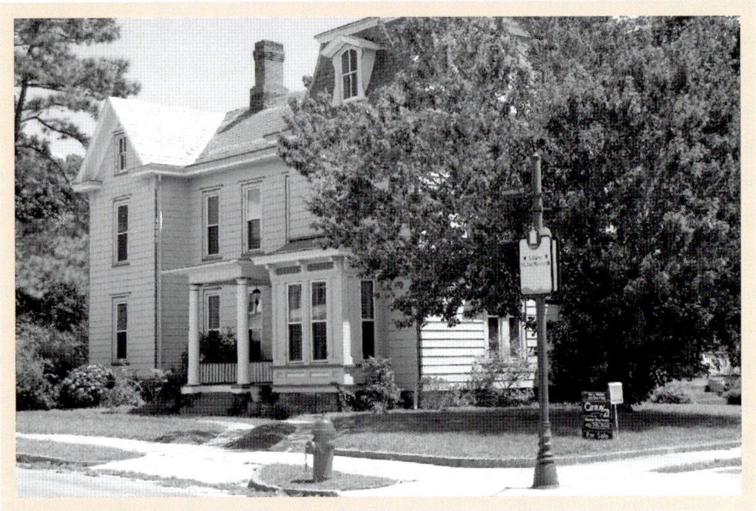

The Hargis-Shockley house was built in 1887 by Ella King Wilson Hargis and Marion Toadvine Hargis. This large L-shaped home has patterned slate shingles and gable roofs, as well as Tuscan-columned porches. The land was originally purchased for $650 from George W. and Ellen Bishop. The home did not leave the Hargis family until 1946, when Samuel Shockley purchased it. Now the property is owned by a lawyer and his wife. There has been a new kitchen put in, and they have renovated the inside of the home. There have been no architectural changes to this home. (Then photograph courtesy of Worcester County Library; now photograph by the author.)

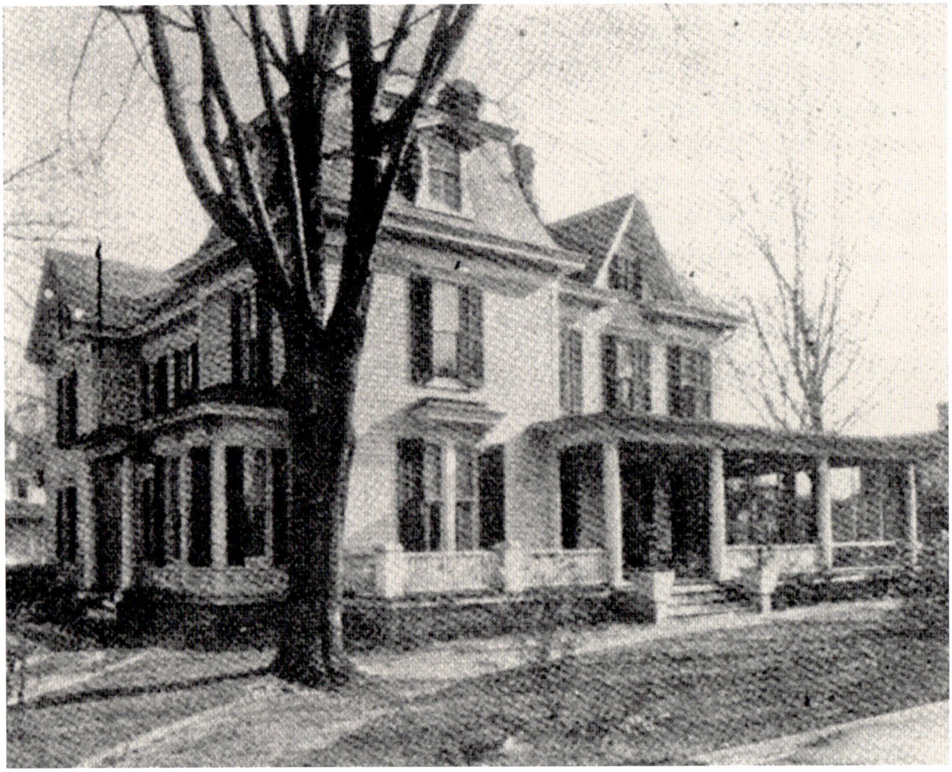

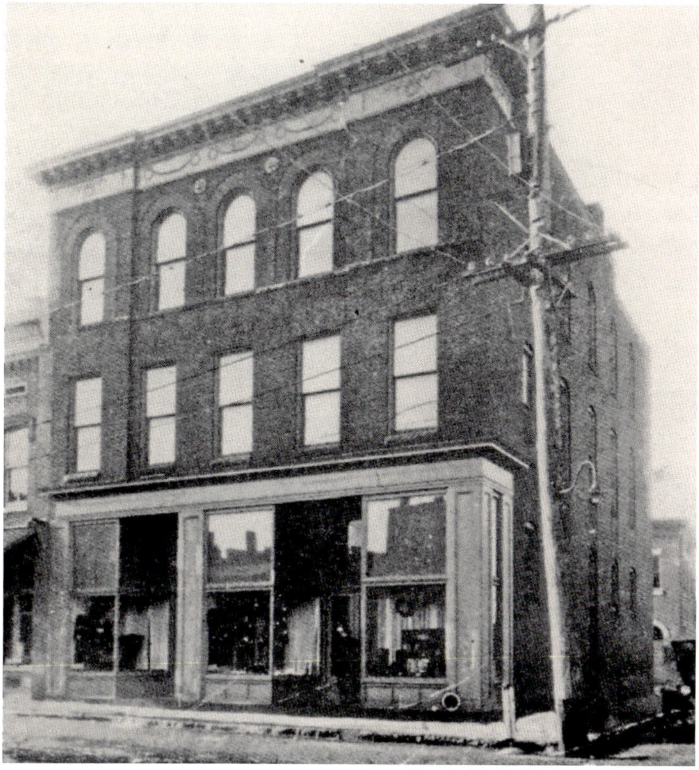

The Masonic lodge is located on the corner of West Green and Pearl Streets in downtown Snow Hill. The approximate date of the building is 1894. For many years, this building housed the A&P grocery store. Now this historic building is home to the Gathering Place, formerly Take Two Scoops. The current owner of the building is real estate agent Gary Weber. (Then photograph courtesy of Worcester County Library; now photograph by the author.)

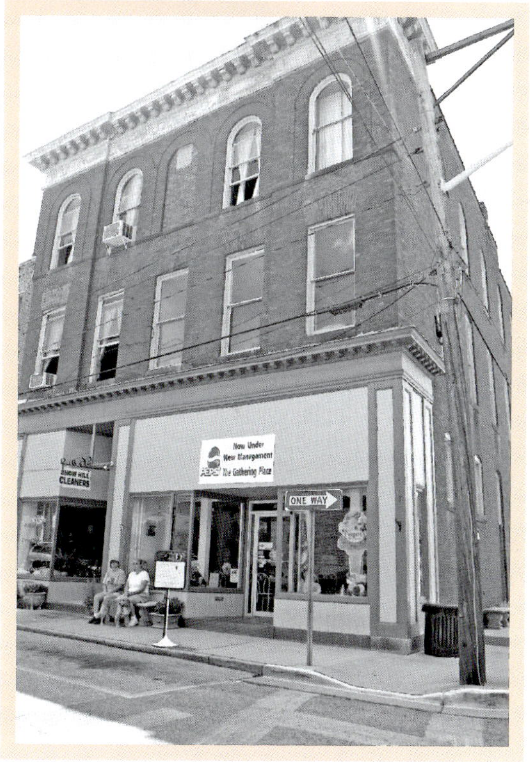

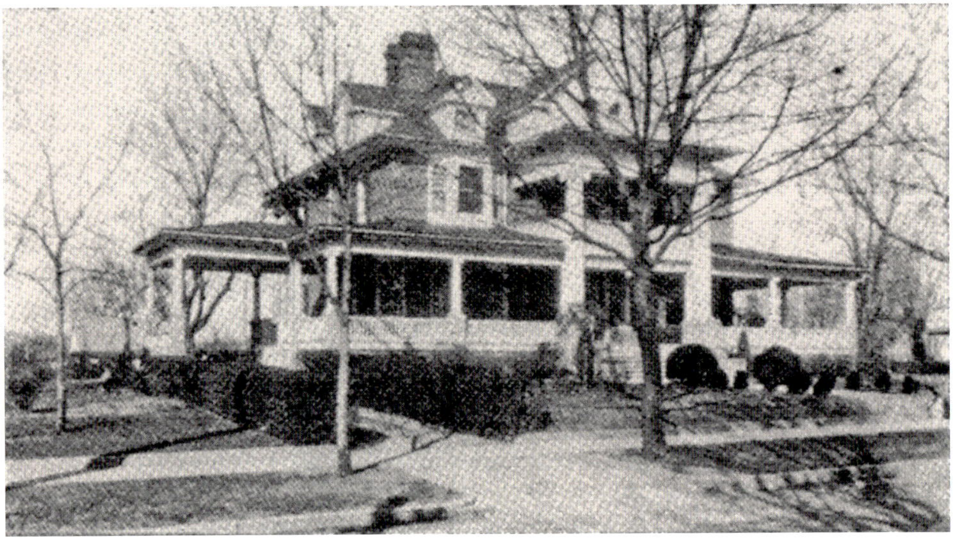

The Oscar M. Purnell house is a Colonial brick home built in 1900 on a triangular lot. The builder and architect are unknown. There was a 20-year lease in 1796 that transferred part of the lot from George Spence to James Givens at an annual rental fee of 25 shillings. James Givens later surfaced in the history of Whatcoat Methodist Church as the treasurer. This building is now occupied by county office space and is undergoing renovation. (Then photograph courtesy of Worcester County Library; now photograph by the author.)

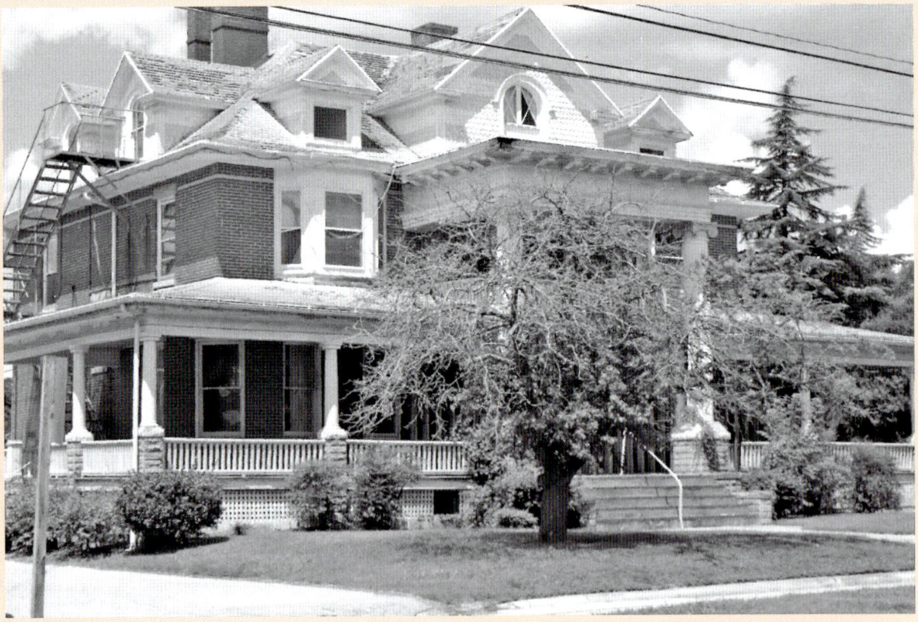

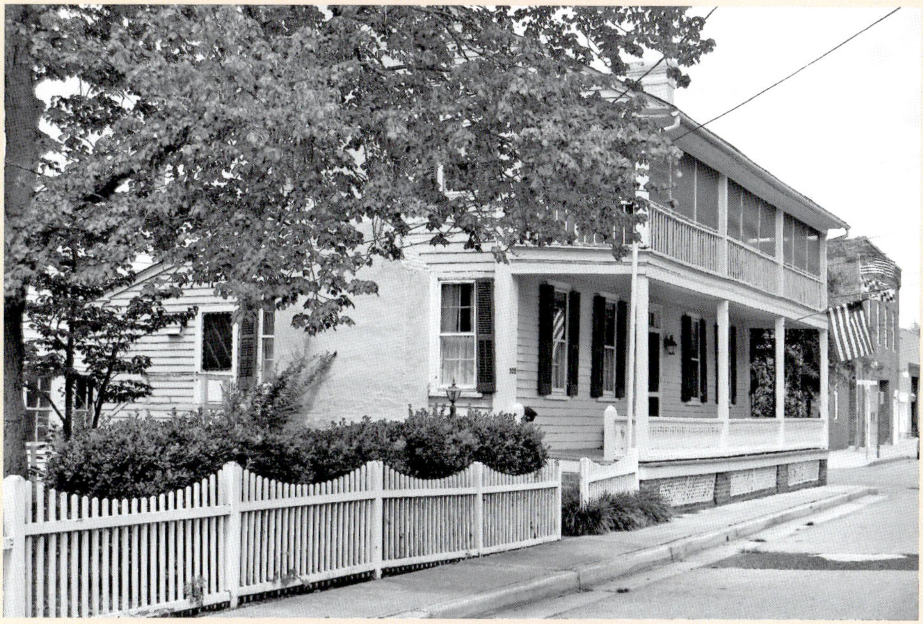

This West Green Street home is fronted by an engaged two-story porch and is two-and-a-half stories high. Built around 1835, the John S. Aydolotte house was originally owned by prominent landowner Levin Townsend, who also had a business interest in the town. Banker Barry Laws is the current owner. Minimal changes have been done to the home to date. (Then photograph courtesy of Worcester County Library; now photograph by the author.)

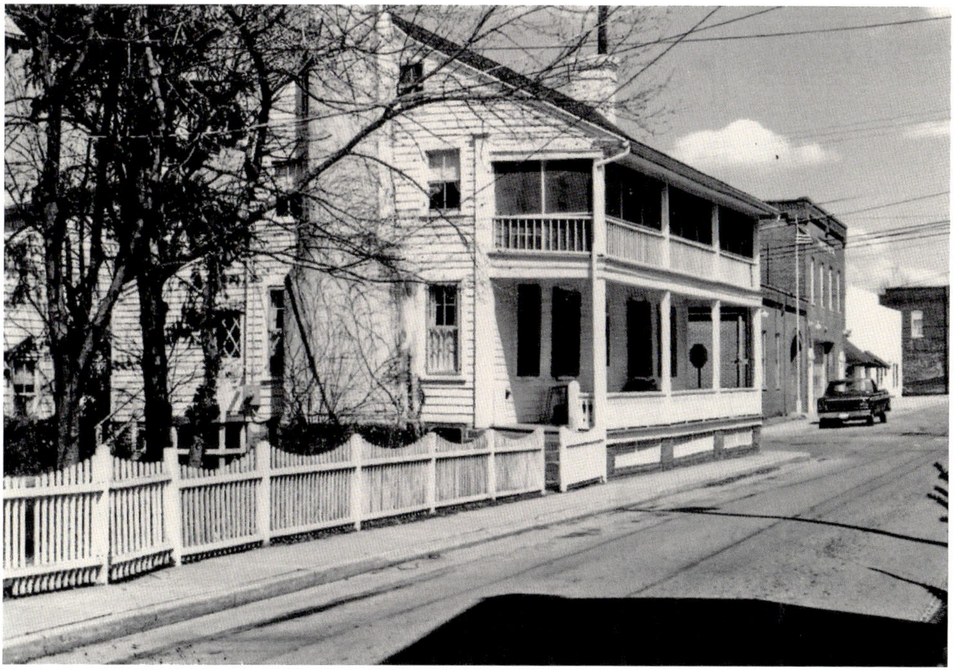

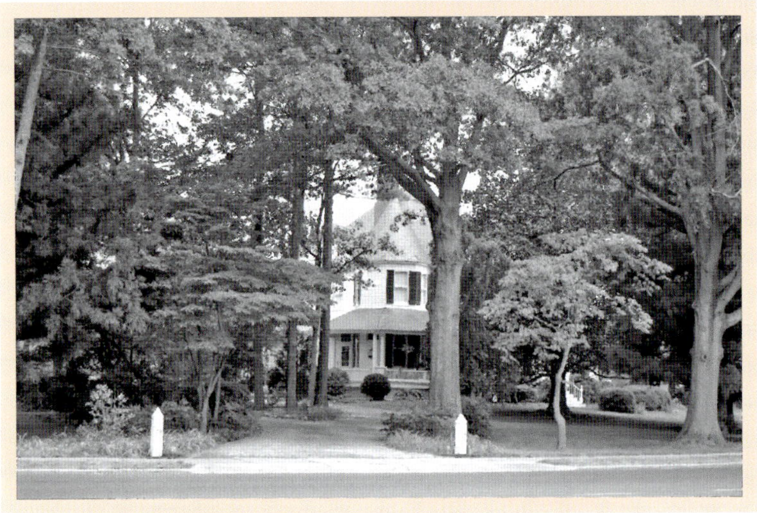

One of the most elaborate Queen Anne–style houses on the Eastern Shore sits in Snow Hill. Built by architect Jackson Gott between 1889 and 1890, the governor's mansion is the largest original home still standing in Snow Hill. The prestigious home has multiple towers covered in slate, gabled dormers, eyebrow-shaped vents, and copper cresting. John Walter Smith, Maryland's governor from 1900 to 1904, lived in this home. He owned a dozen farms and owned shares of two western Maryland lumber companies. As with many homes in Snow Hill, the governor's mansion had many owners. It is now owned by Kemp Wills. (Then photograph courtesy of Worcester County Library; now photograph by the author.)

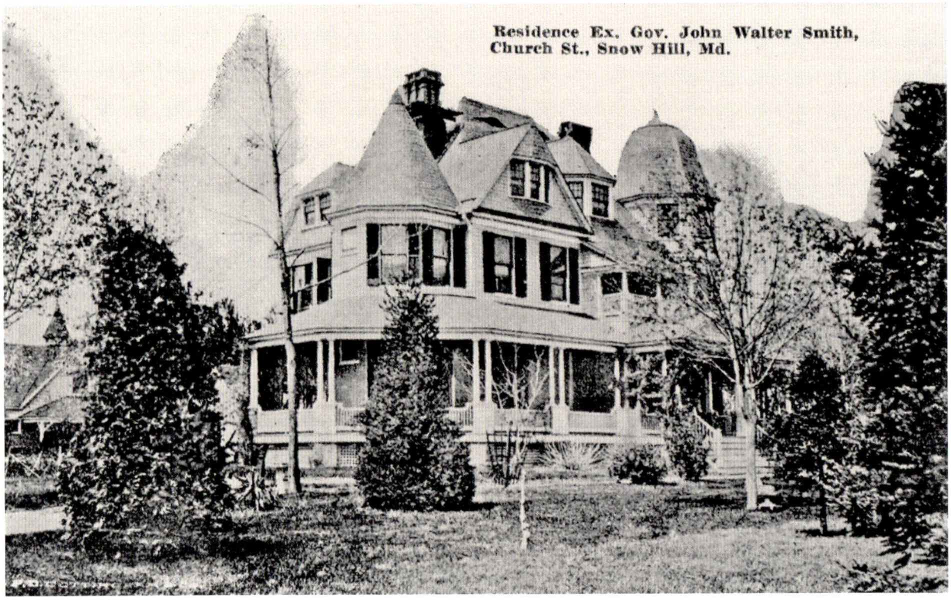

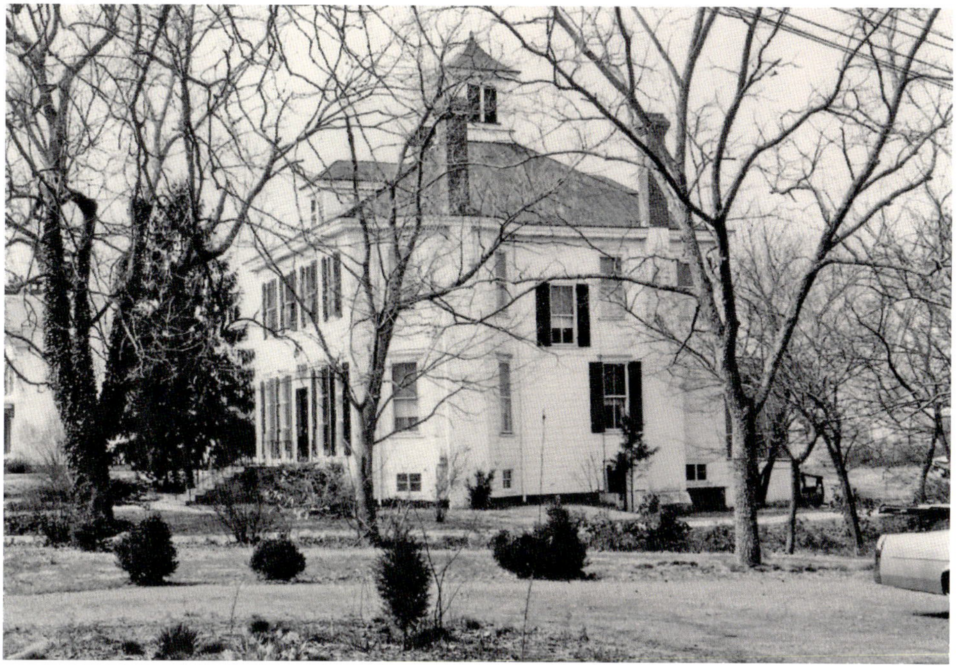

This unusual home, the Alfred Pinchin house, was built around 1882 and gives character to West Federal Street, combining mid- to late-19th century styles, whereas the other homes show more distinct time-period styles. The Pinchin house served as a Presbyterian manse until 1950. The home has been well preserved by the current owners, and its caretakers are Dick and Kristen DeAngelis. (Then photograph courtesy of Worcester County Library; now photograph by the author.)

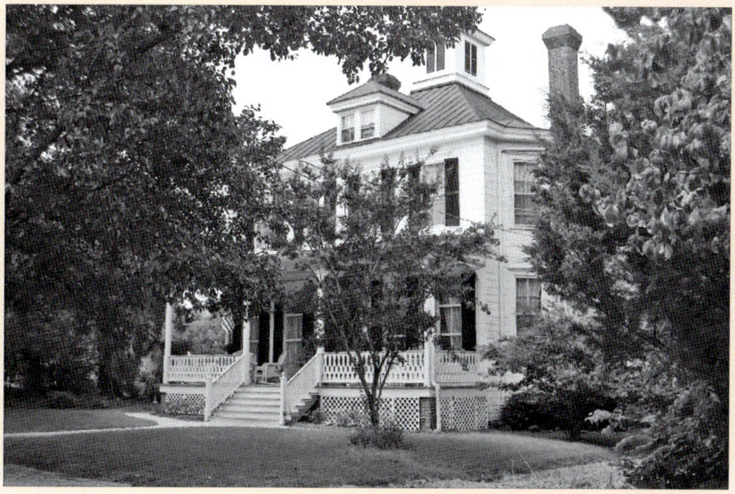

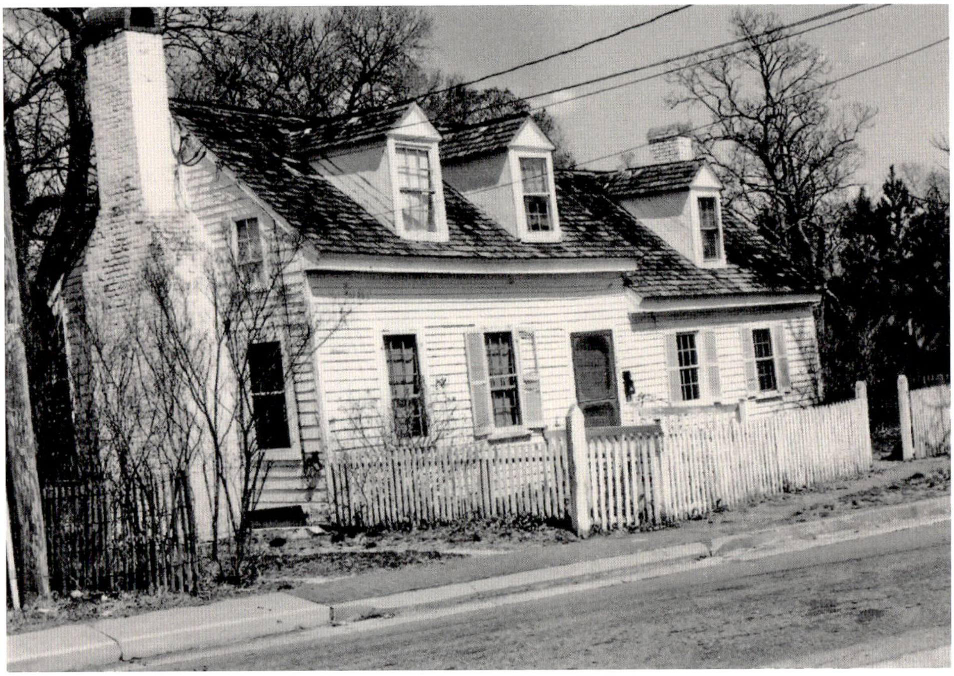

Rumored to be one of the town's oldest homes, the John Blair house is on a small lot on Green Street neighboring the River house. This one-and-a-half story dwelling was built in 1835 by John Blair, but little else is known about him. This home was assigned No. 1 on the earliest Snow Hill land plat. Today the John Blair house is home to the Adcock Studio art gallery. (Then photograph courtesy of Worcester County Library; now photograph by the author.)

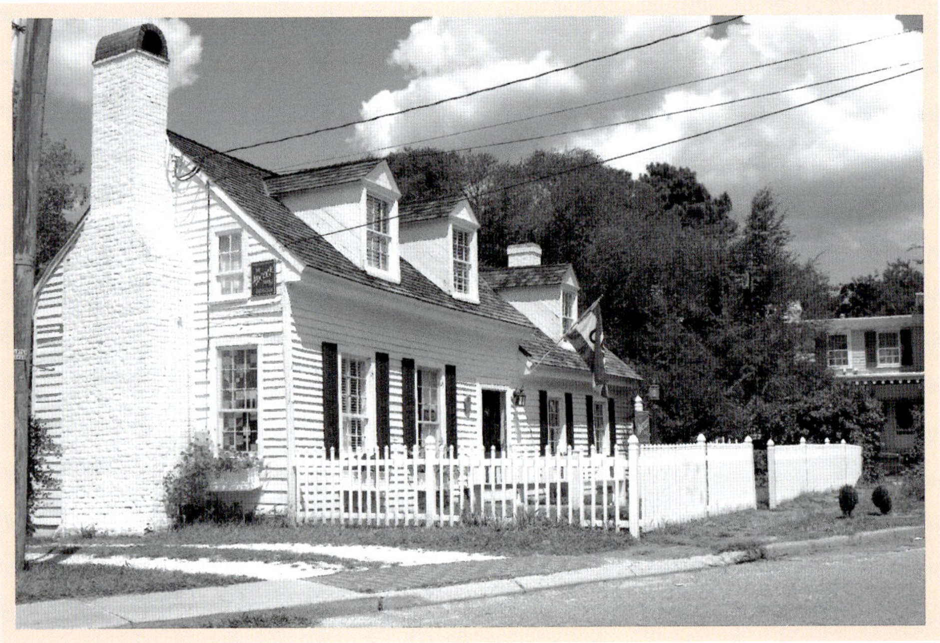

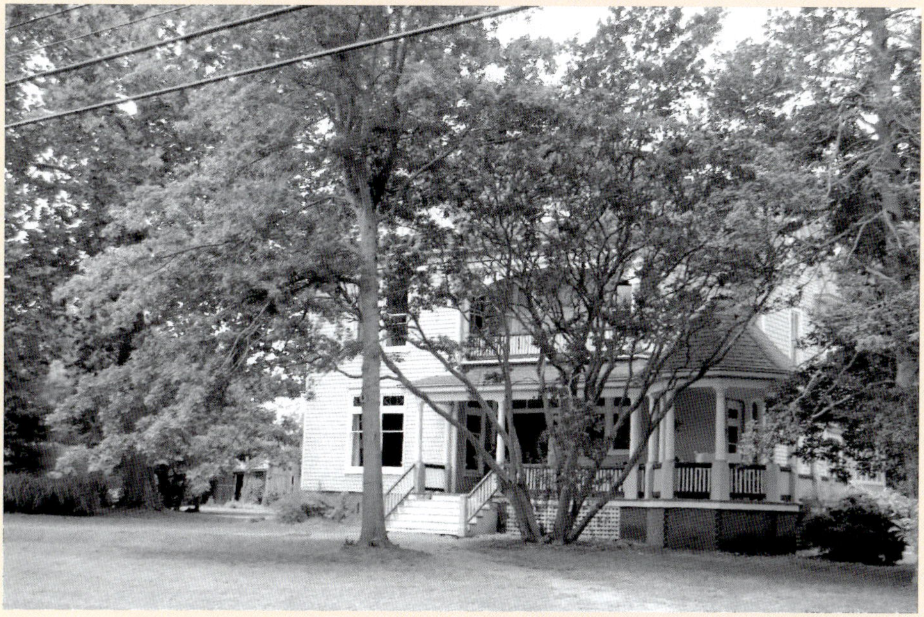

Longtime attorney and author Clayton J. Purnell purchased the land this home is built on in 1894 for $1,100. Soon afterwards, he appointed architect Jackson Gott, the same architect who built the governor's mansion, to erect this spacious home. Unlike the governor's mansion, this home is separated into numerous apartments. The wraparound porch was later removed to accommodate separate living space. Today the property is owned by Dale Evans of Snow Hill, and the apartments are individually leased. (Then photograph courtesy of Worcester County Library; now photograph by the author.)

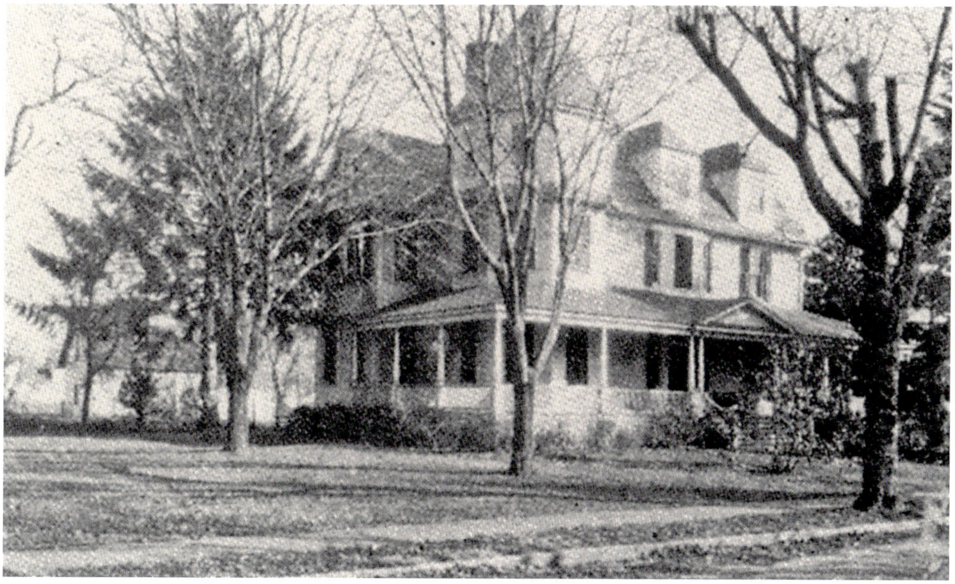

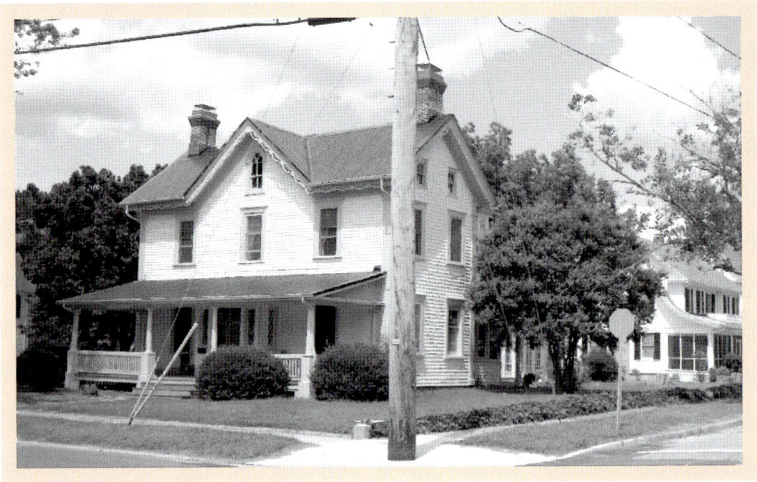

The P. D. Cottingham house sits on the corner lot of Church and Federal Streets. It was built in 1873 for Cottingham, the town druggist. The two-and-a-half story frame home has cross gables and eaves decorated with Victorian sawn work. It was sold by Cottingham's daughters, Priscie and Annie, to W. D. Corrdry in 1906 for $2,800. Today the home is still erect and has had a few architectural changes. (Then photograph courtesy of Worcester County Library; now photograph by the author.)

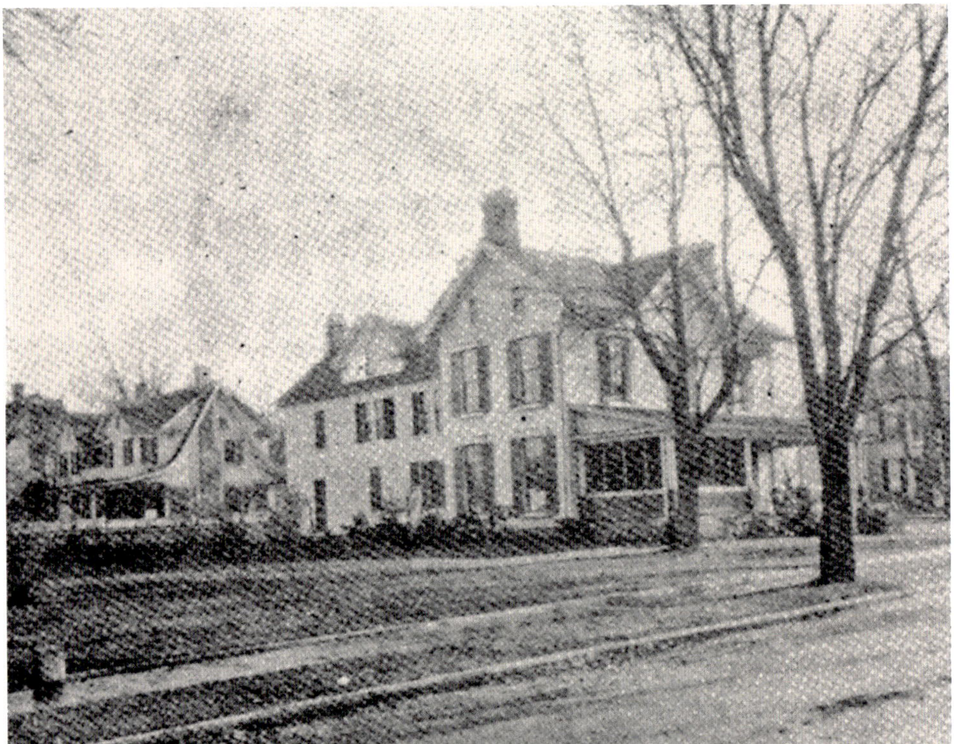

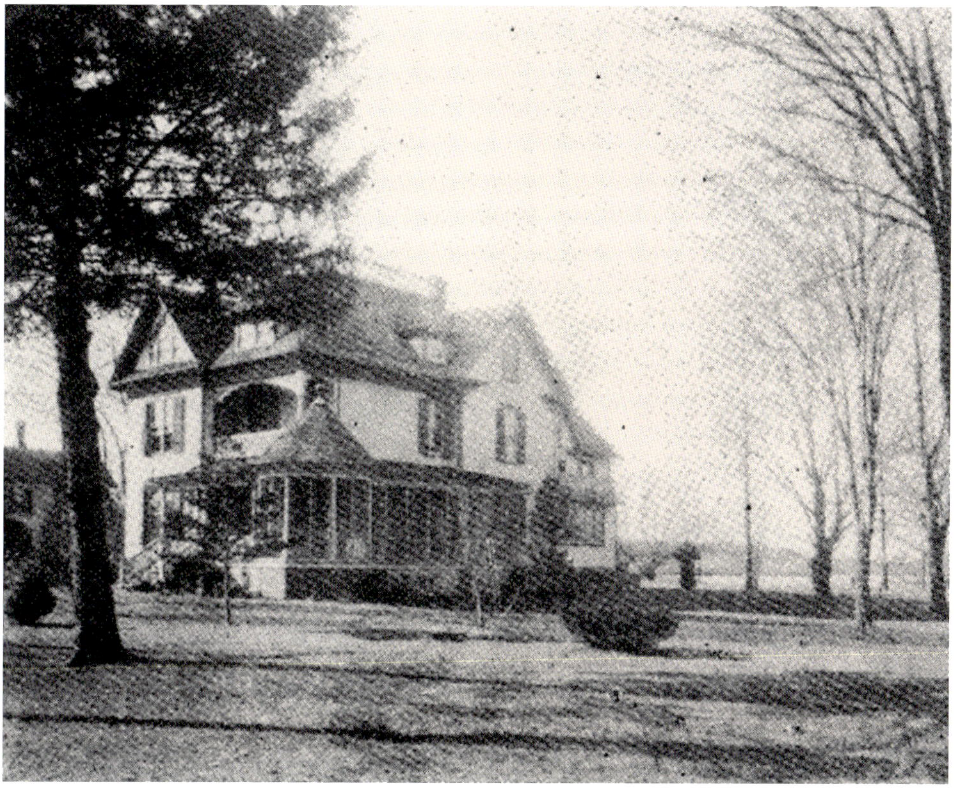

The large Victorian Queen Anne–style Collins Vincent house stands on a generous lot off West Market Street in Snow Hill, overlooking the Pocomoke River. Also know as the Crocker house, this home includes a wraparound porch, projecting gable-roofed pavilions, and colored-glass windows. Today the Collins Vincent house is owned by the Hilliard family and has been updated inside and out. (Then photograph courtesy of Worcester County Library; now photograph by the author.)

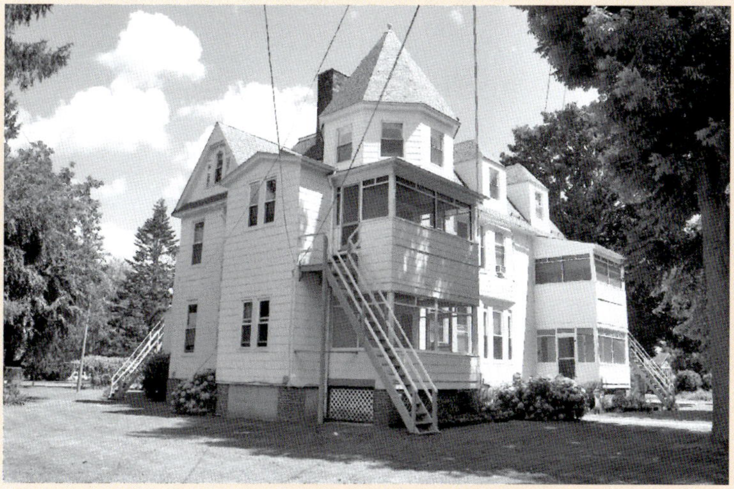

Chanceford Hall is claimed to be the second or third home built in Snow Hill. It once sat on 35 acres of farmland. The land was purchased by James Rownd from Francis Rosse on April 13, 1792, for 100 shillings. Today the inside of the home has been slightly updated and is furnished to reflect the period in which the house was built. The home is now being operated as a bed-and-breakfast. (Then photograph courtesy of Worcester County Library; now photograph by the author.)

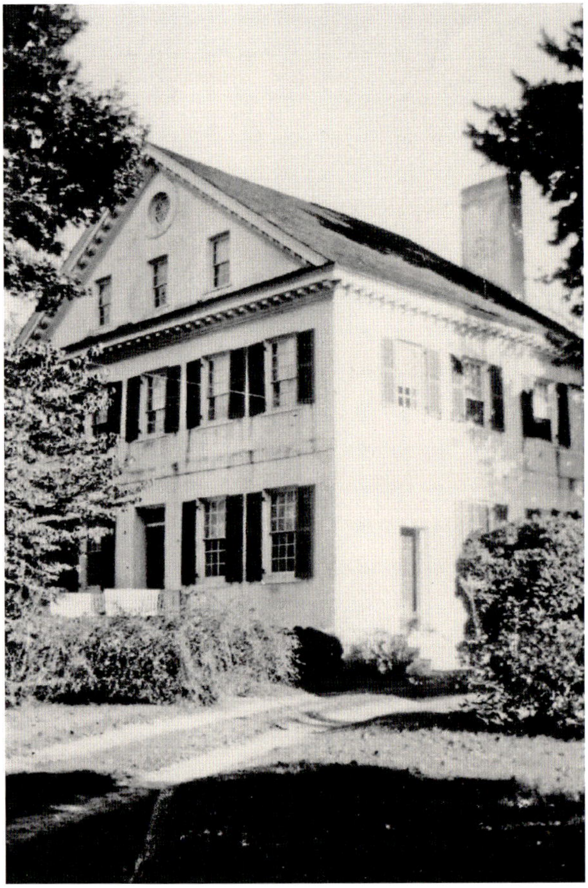

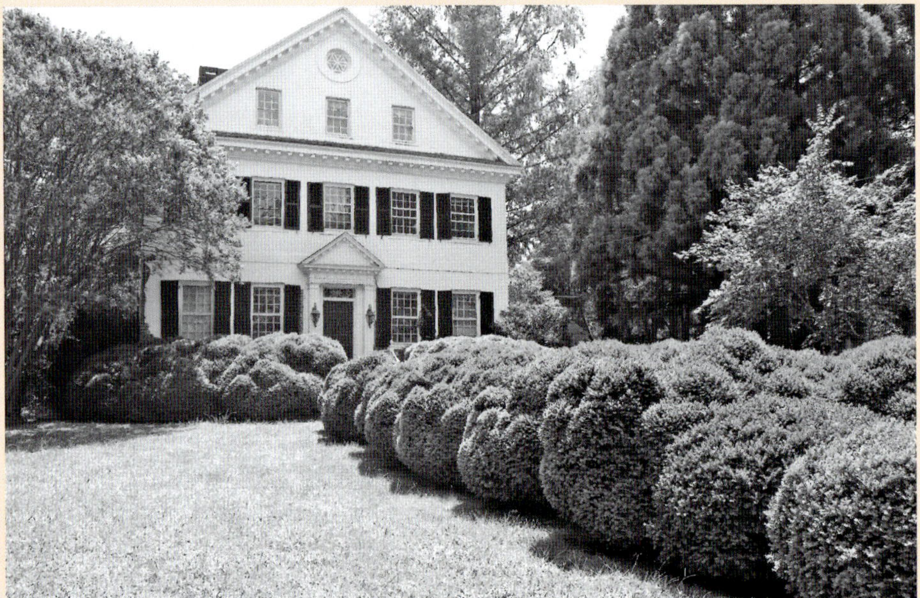

CHAPTER 5

FINANCE AND TRADE

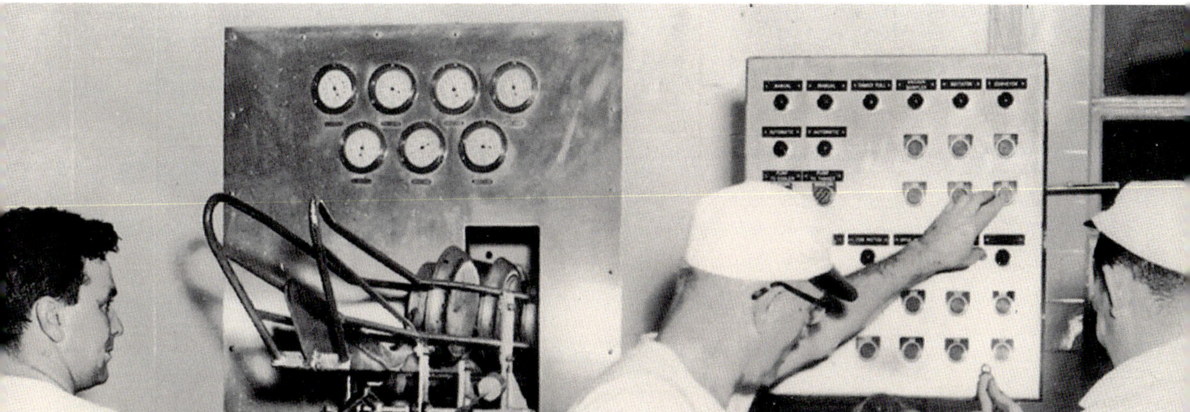

The Philadelphia Dairy Products Receiving Plant on Belt Street in Snow Hill is where dairy farmers brought their milk daily to be tested and cooled for shipment by tanker truck to Philadelphia for processing. The plant closed in the early 1960s. Today the building is used as storage and is on the market for sale. This building would make a great artist studio. (Courtesy of Shirley McWilliams.)

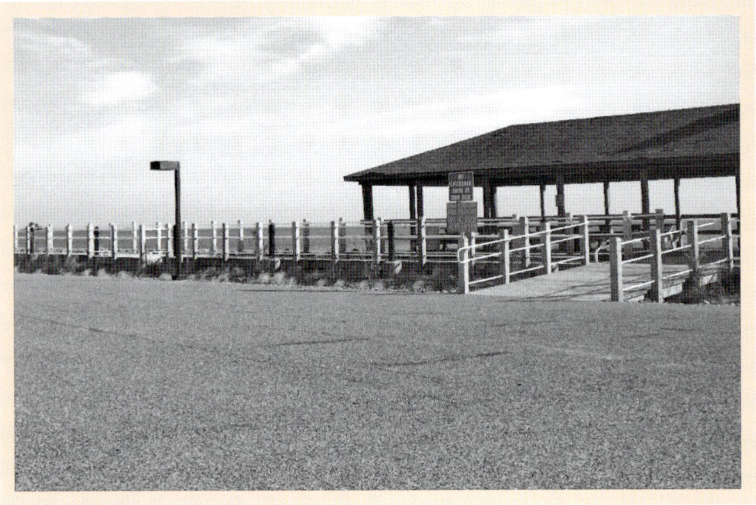

Purnell's Soda Fountain is shown below in the 1930s. It was one of the many reasons to visit Public Landing. Sadly, it was destroyed in 1933, when it was hit by a hurricane that swept most of the buildings into the bay. Today the only thing left at Public Landing is a pier for boating and crabbing, and in the summer, there is a sliding board that is put up for swimmers to enjoy. The Public Landing is a nice place to spend the day on the water. (Then photograph courtesy of Worcester County Library; now photograph by the author.)

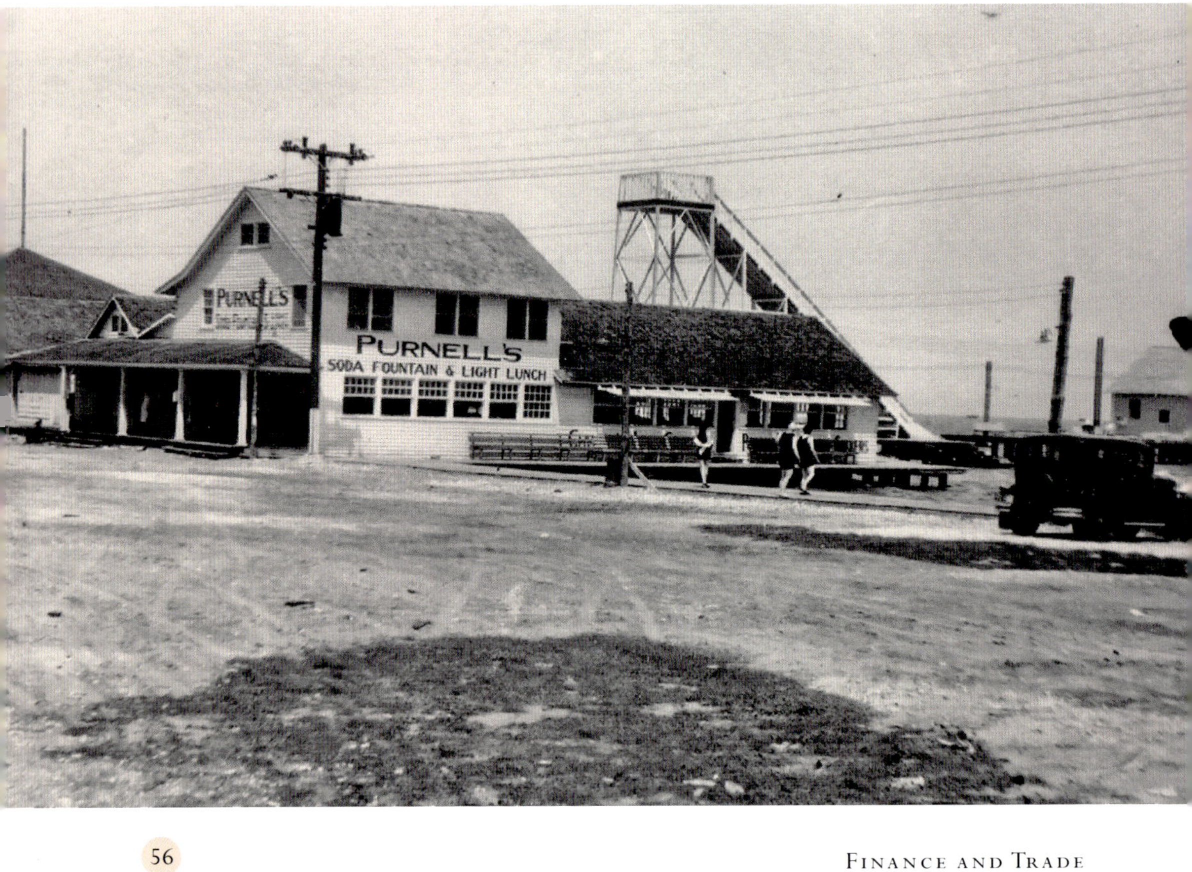

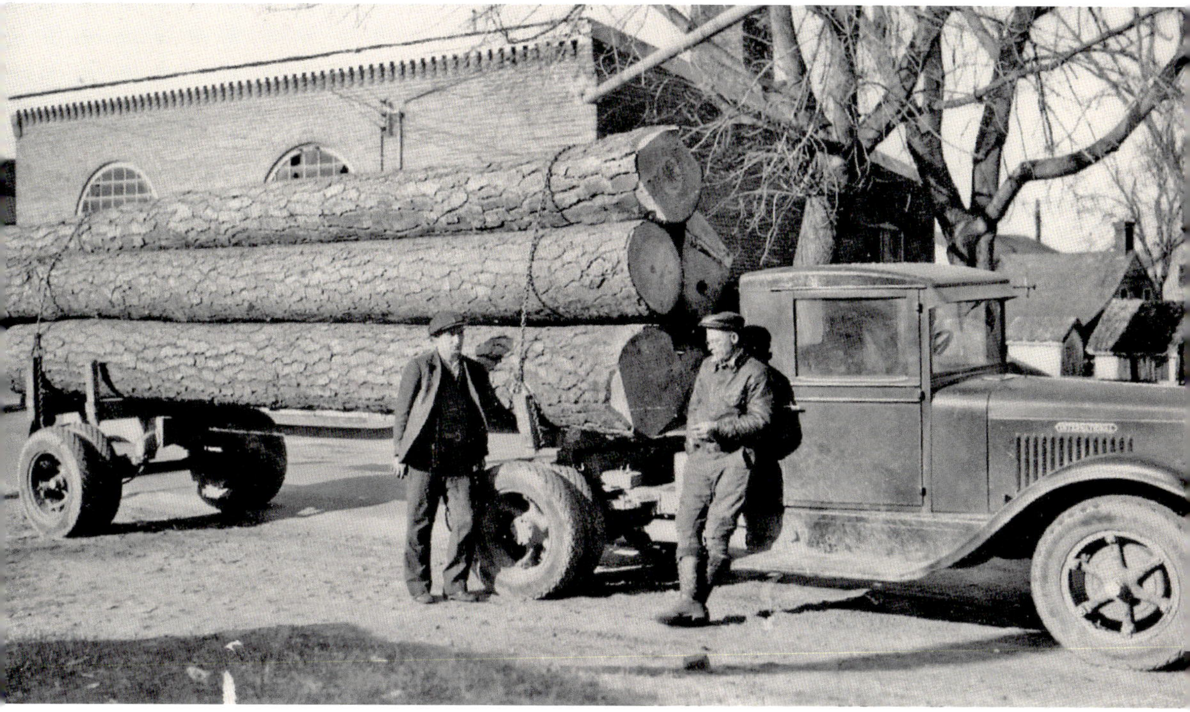

Shown above are two employees from the Paul Jones Lumber Company, which was established in 1918. Becoming the third largest supplier of timber products, this lumber company was responsible for supplying poles and pilings for the 1939 New York World's Fair. Still owned and operated by the Jones family, Paul M. Jones Lumber Company produces lumber to be shipped all around. The company is one of two mills in the Snow Hill area. (Then photograph courtesy of Worcester county library; now photograph taken by Michelle C Fulton.)

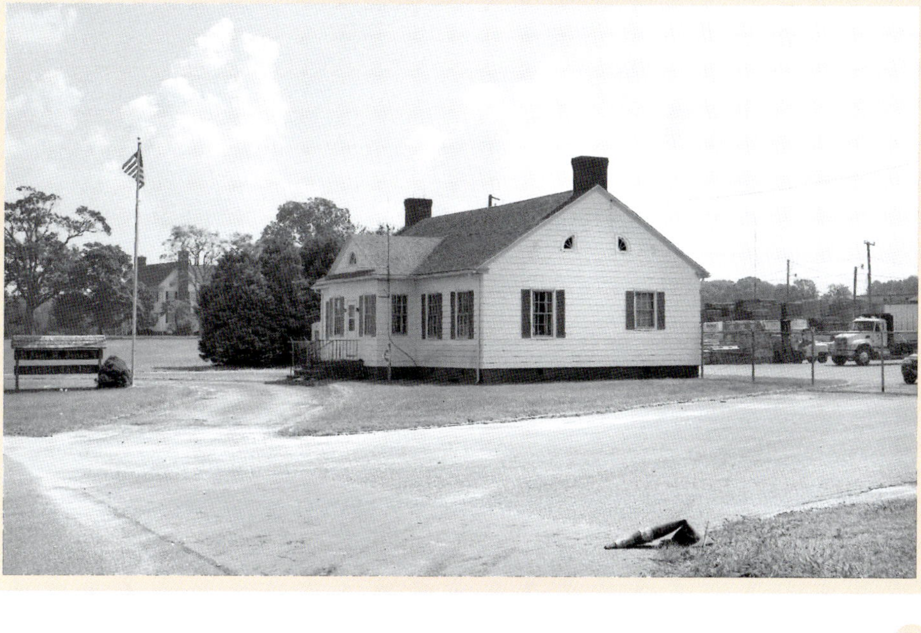

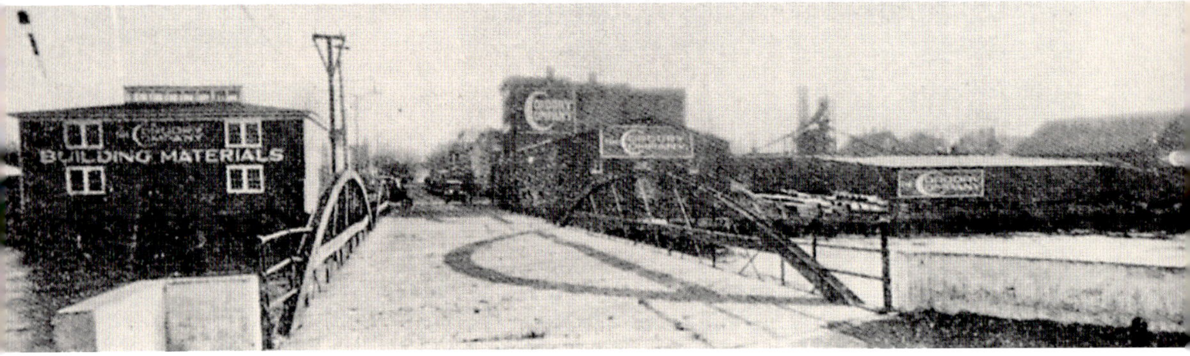

The Snow Hill Bridge is the only entrance into Snow Hill from Salisbury. Pictured above in the 1920s, one can see numerous buildings that made up the Corddry Company, established in 1883. Built along the river and therefore perfect for exports, the Corddry Company cut and manufactured lumber, boxes, and building materials. It soon grew to include a storage facility, hardware store, and coal yard. Today two of the buildings remain, occupied by the Pocomoke River Canoe Company, owned by Barry Laws, and the Worcester County extension office. Along the same street there is now a P&C Bank, Sturgis Park, and parking for library and bank employees and the Worcester county extension office. (Then photograph courtesy of Worcester County Library; now photograph by the author.)

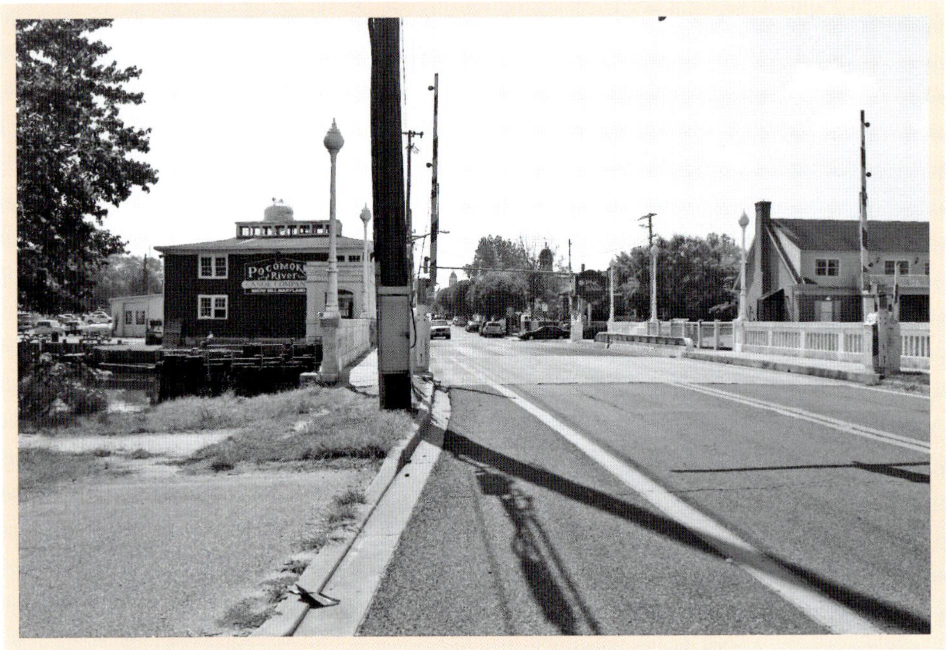

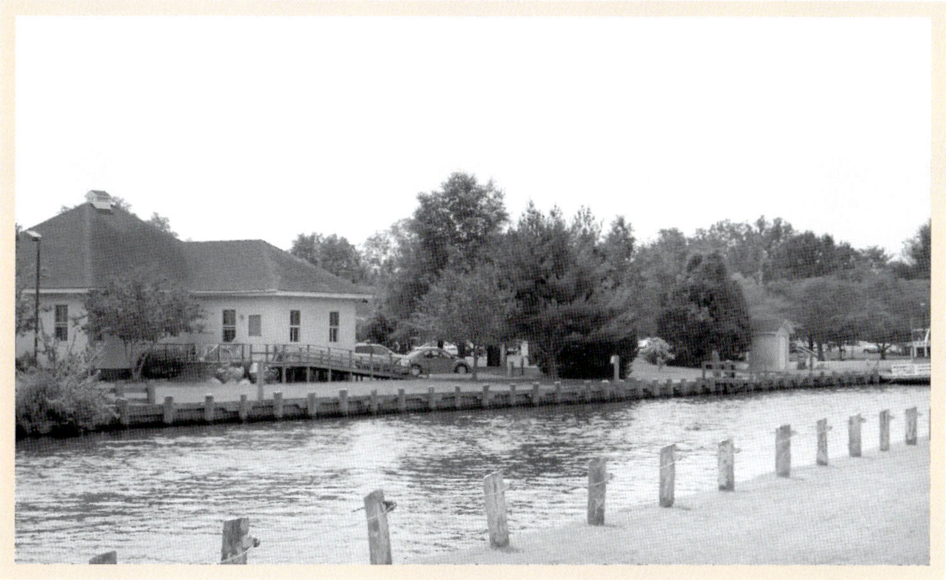

The picture below shows the *Mabel* leaving the pier in Snow Hill. It was used to carry the mail to Pocomoke. The people who lived nearby would gather outside their houses to watch the *Mabel* come and go. Today this pier has been updated, and Sturgis Park meets up to it on the Pocomoke River. (Then photograph courtesy of Worcester County Library; now photograph by the author.)

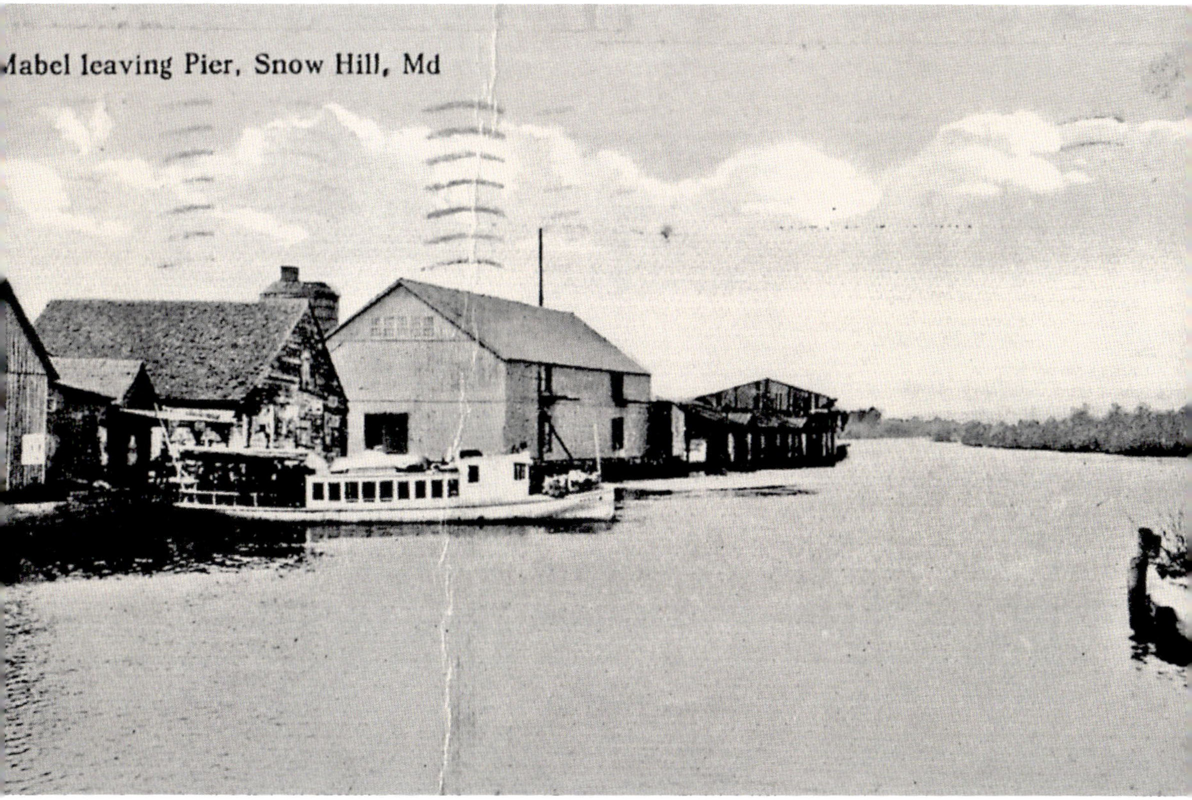

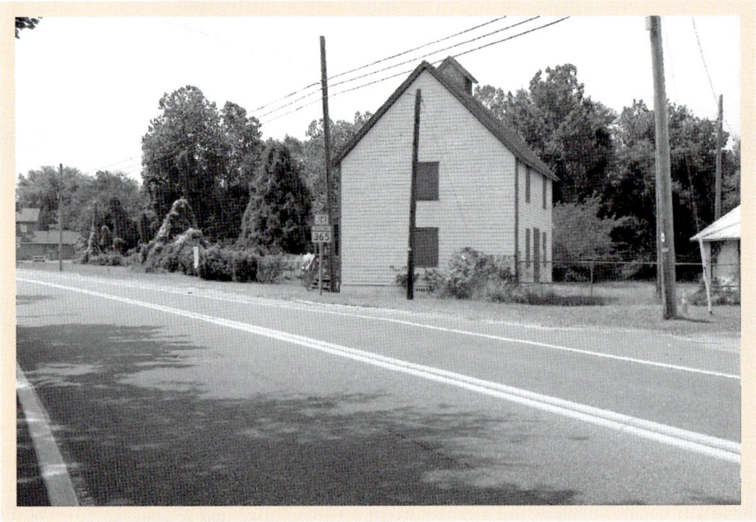

The picture below shows the Old Snow Hill Potato House, built in 1913. This two-story building was the location for the storage of the area's sweet potato harvests. It was ideal for transporting goods because it was built next to the railroads as well as Market Street, the main road through Snow Hill. Besides the loss of the chimney, the building has not been altered since the early 20th century. The potato house is now owned by Gary Weber and is not in use. (Then photograph courtesy of Worcester County Library; now photograph by the author.)

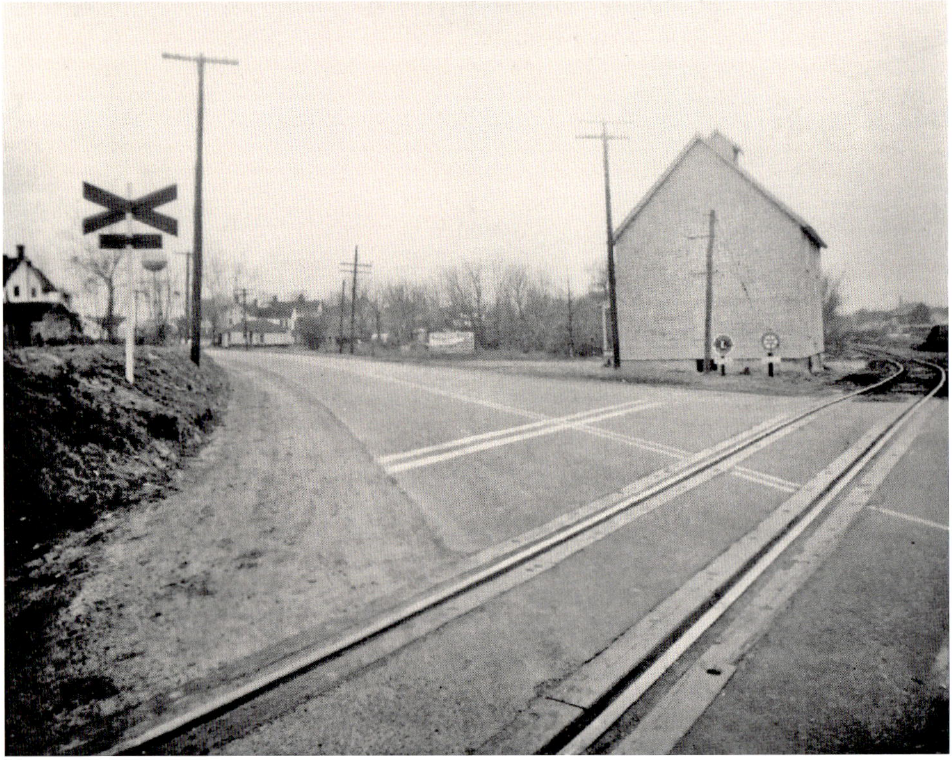

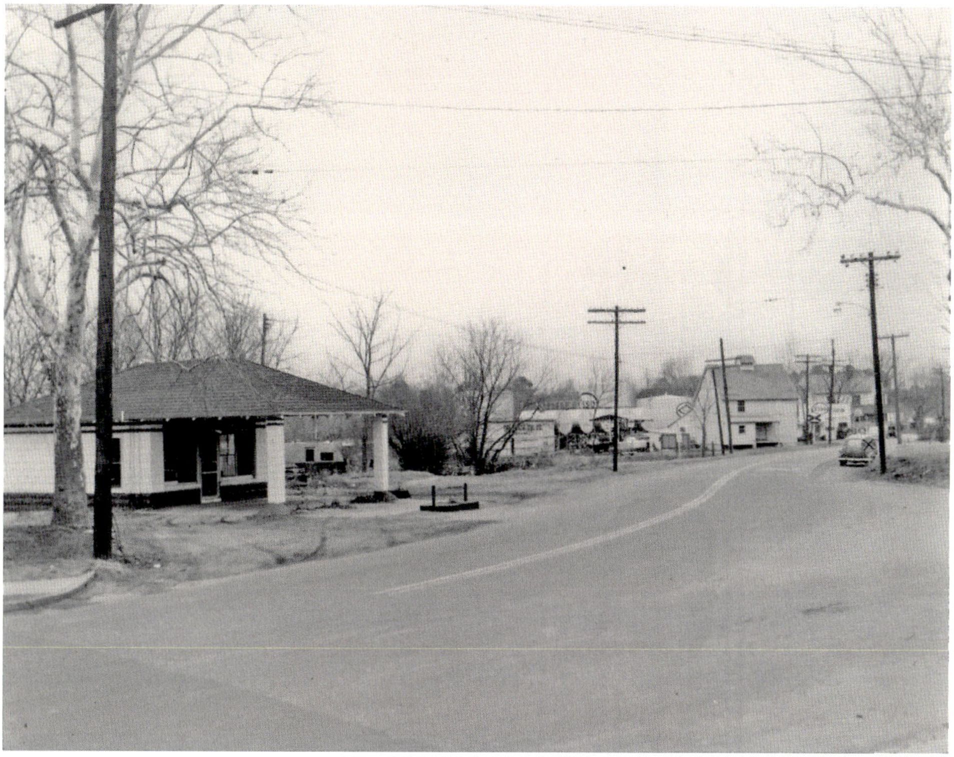

Built in 1908, the old Snow Hill Potato House is a familiar architectural feature of the lower shore of Maryland. It was built for storage of the sweet potato crops in the early 19th century and was easily accessed by the railroad for the crop's export. The original owners of the building are unknown. Today this building is used for general storage, and all open areas are now covered by blue shutters. (Then photograph courtesy of Worcester County Library; now photograph by the author.)

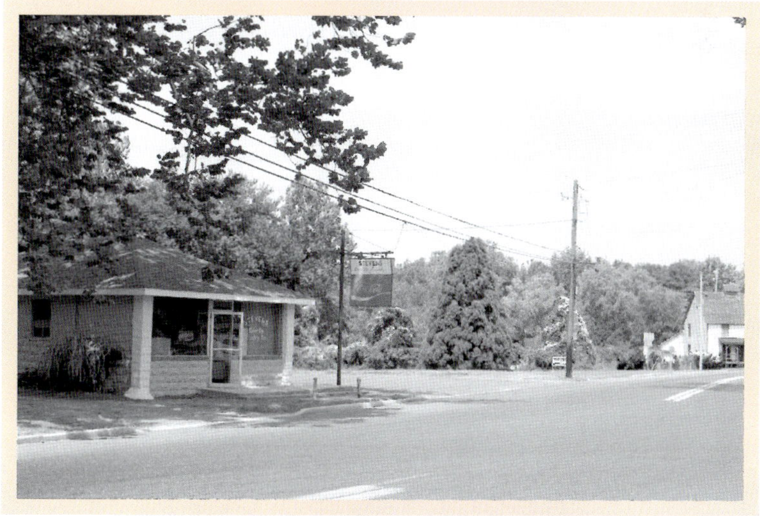

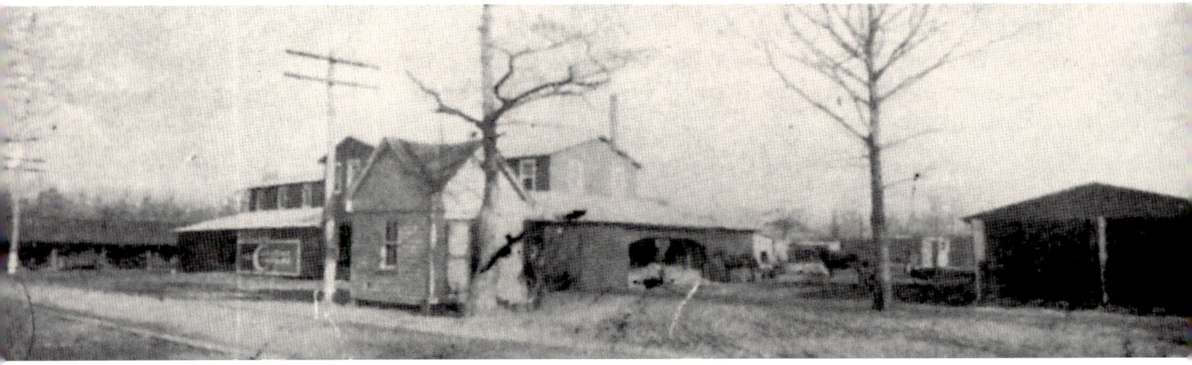

Established in 1883, the Corddry Company was originally named William D. Corddry and Sons. The company cut and manufactured boxes, lumber, and building materials, and was on the riverbank, making it easy to export items. The Corddry Company grew and eventually included a hardware store, storage facilities, and a coal yard. The only building still standing is the building materials structure, now owned by Barry Laws. It is now a canoe rental shop. (Then photograph courtesy of Worcester County Library; now photograph by the author.)

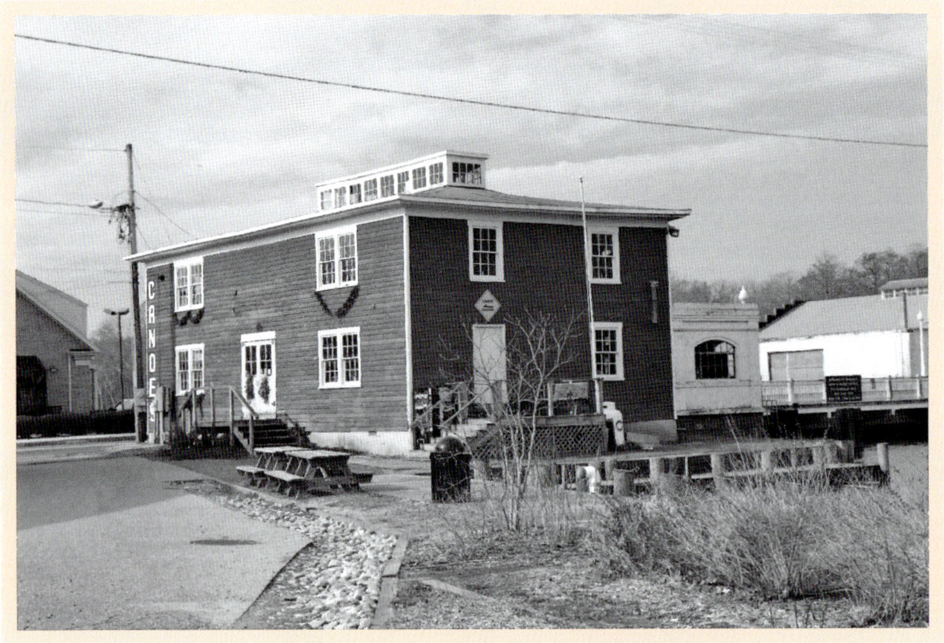

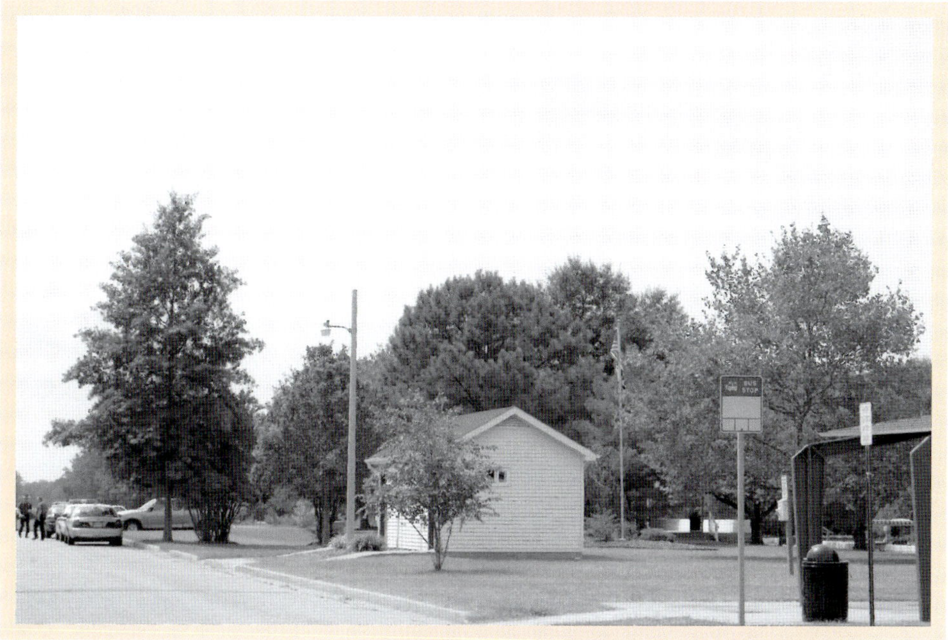

The early-1930s photograph below shows the Worcester Fertilizer Company. The schooners were used to import the raw materials used to make the fertilizer from Baltimore. The fertilizer manufactured here was used not only in Snow Hill, but also in six other neighboring counties. The Worcester Fertilizer Company is no longer here. (Then photograph courtesy of Worcester County Library; now photograph by the author.)

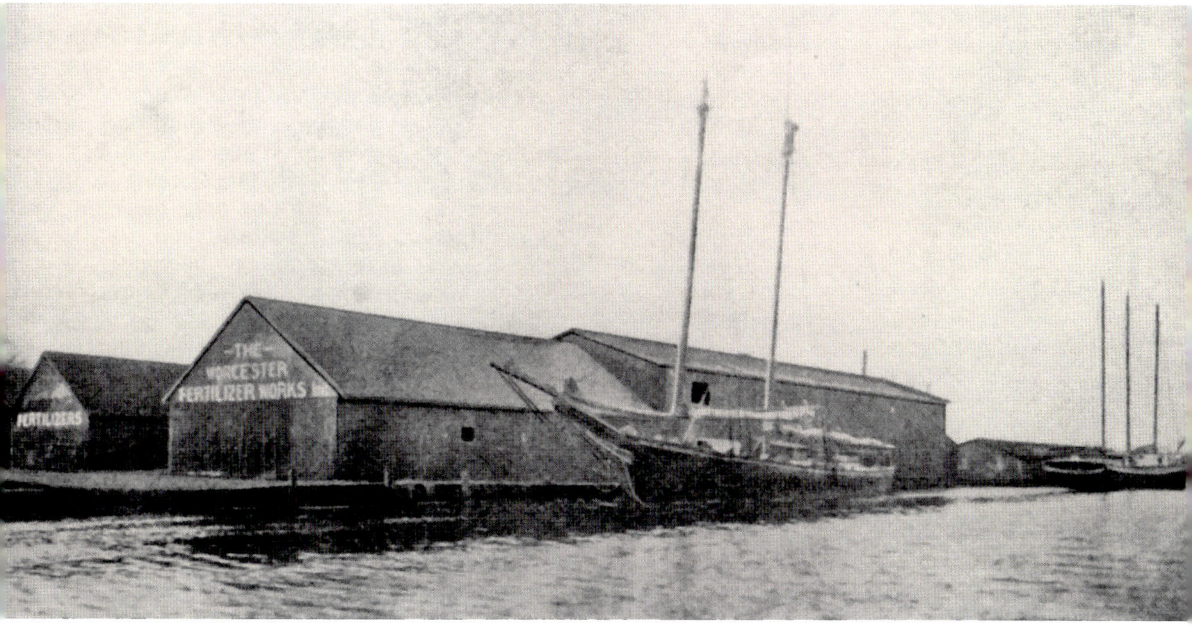

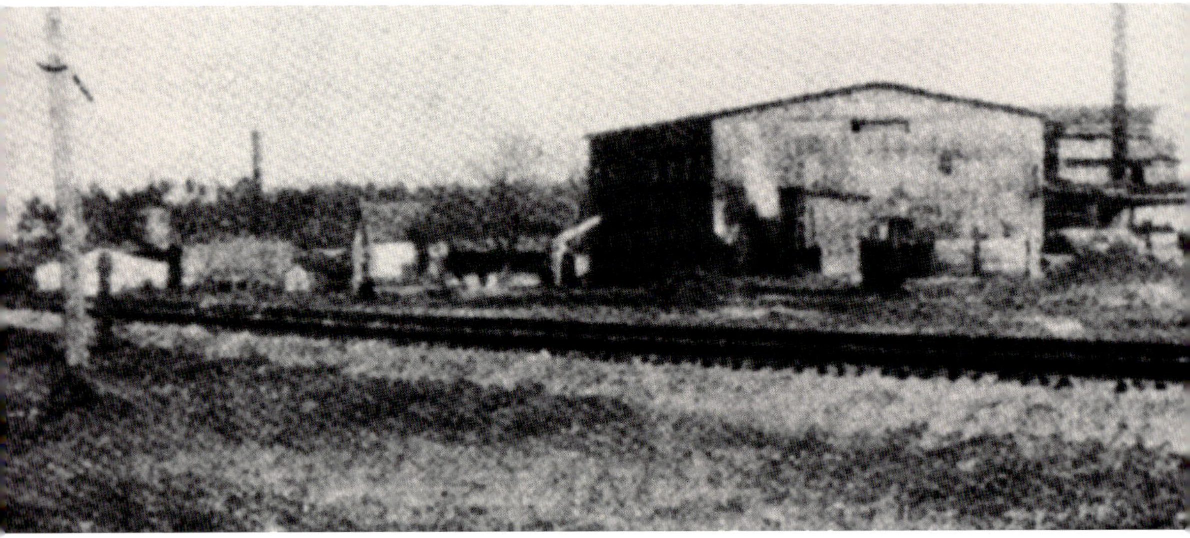

Established in 1870, the Richardson Smith and Moore Company was one of the principal lumber mills in Worcester County. Its owners also had gristmills and sawmills in Virginia and North Carolina. At the beginning of the 20th century, the business employed between 900 and 1,000 employees and brought in around $1 million each year making boxes, baskets, and lumber. Today

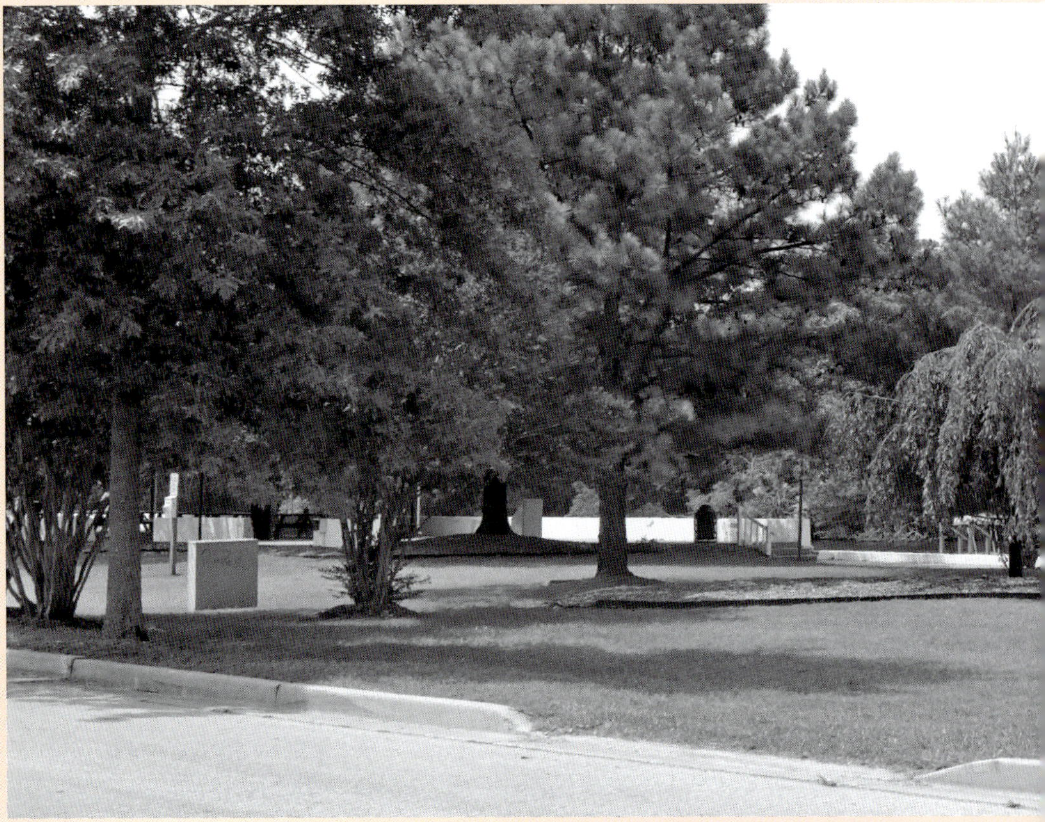

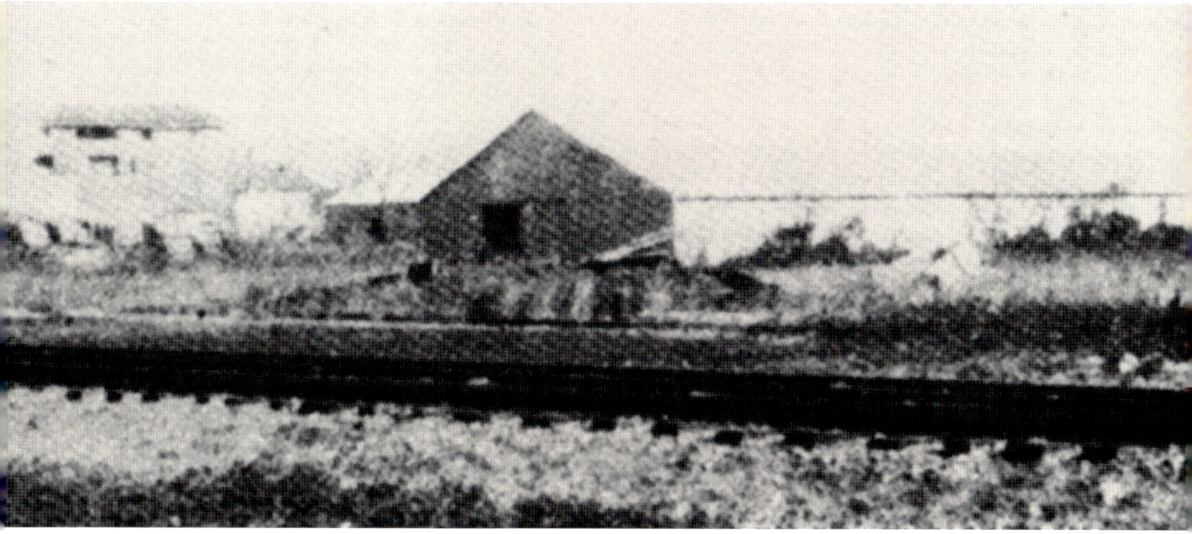

the property, which lines the Pocomoke River, is Sturgis Park. The main area has a pavilion with tables and is used for many events, including weddings, dances, and the annual Fourth of July celebration, which is sponsored by the town. (Then photograph courtesy of Worcester County Library; now photograph by the author.)

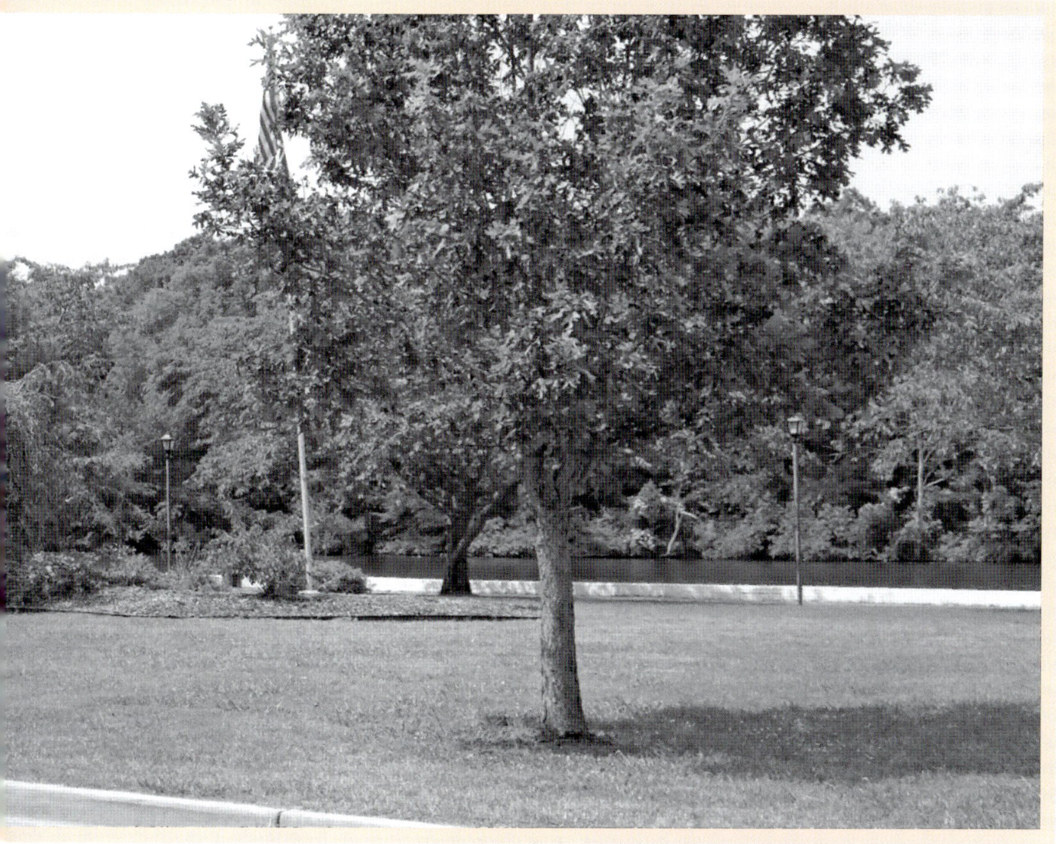

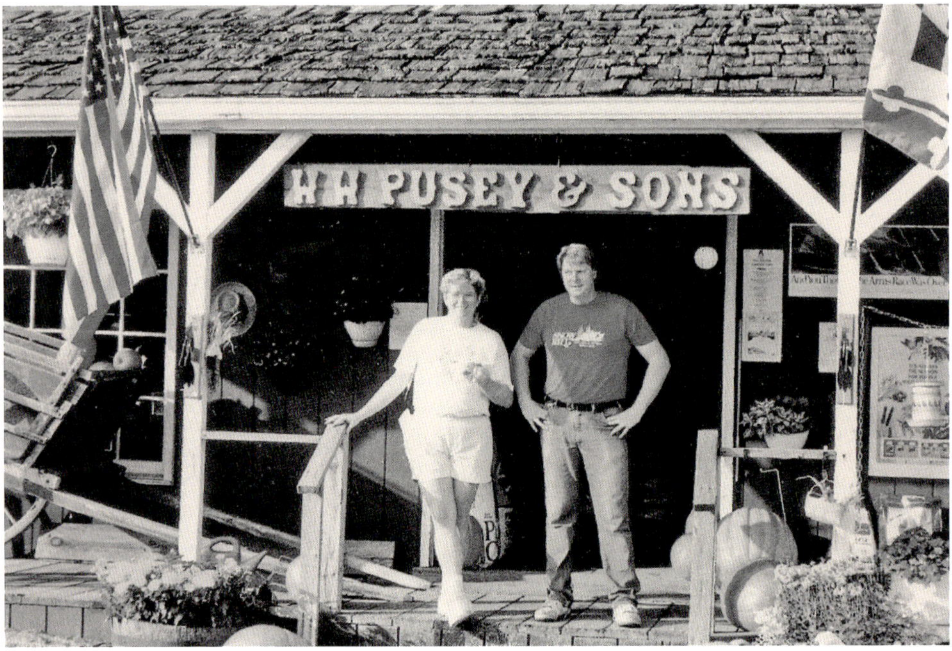

Pusey's Country Store was originally built for farm machinery, sales, and services in the early 1930s. In 1970, William W. Pusey took ownership and turned it into a Southern States co-op. Later the family dropped the Southern States name and became independent. Pusey's is owned and operated now by William W. Pusey's children, Pat, Danny, and Cindy Pusey. Pusey's has an array of items including Maryland wines, cheeses, ice cream, numerous microbrew beers, locally canned soups, and McCuchteon's products. Stop by anytime and meet Rosebud the cat, who lives at the store. Cindy and Danny Pusey are pictured in both images. (Then photograph courtesy of Worcester County Library; now photograph by the author.)

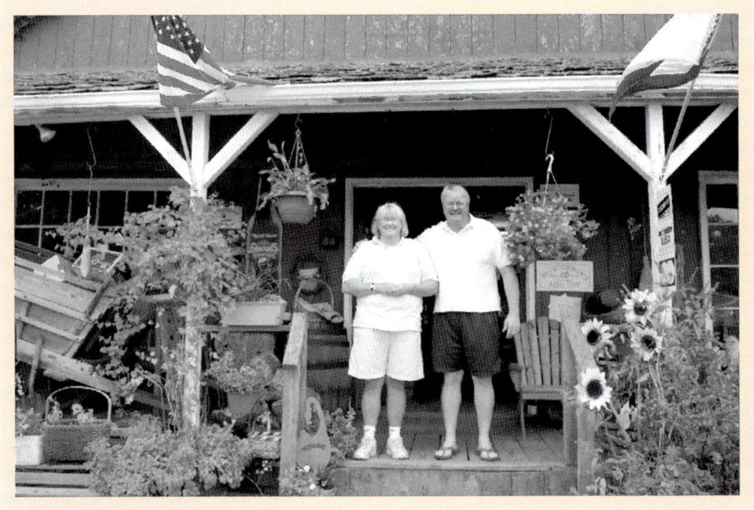

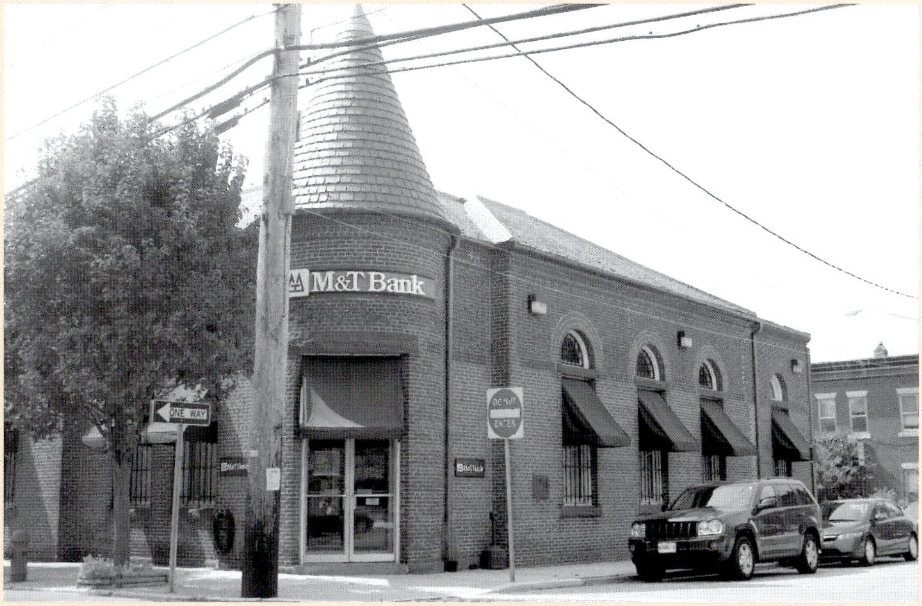

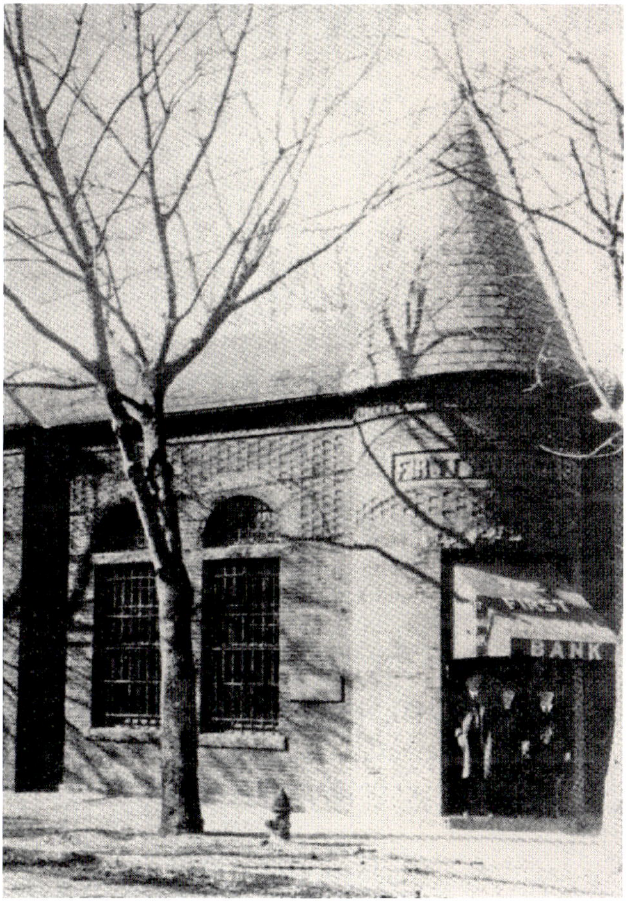

Gov. John Walter Smith opened the First National Bank on September 12, 1887, with an initial investment of $50,000. This building stands on the corner of Bank and Market Streets. It is the longest operating financial institution in Worcester County. The bank offices were temporarily relocated to the courthouse-yard law office of Clayton J. Purnell due to damage from the fire in August 1893. Today the bank is called First Shore Federal. The structure of the bank has been updated dramatically. It is now a single-level building. (Then photograph courtesy of Worcester County Library; now photograph by the author.)

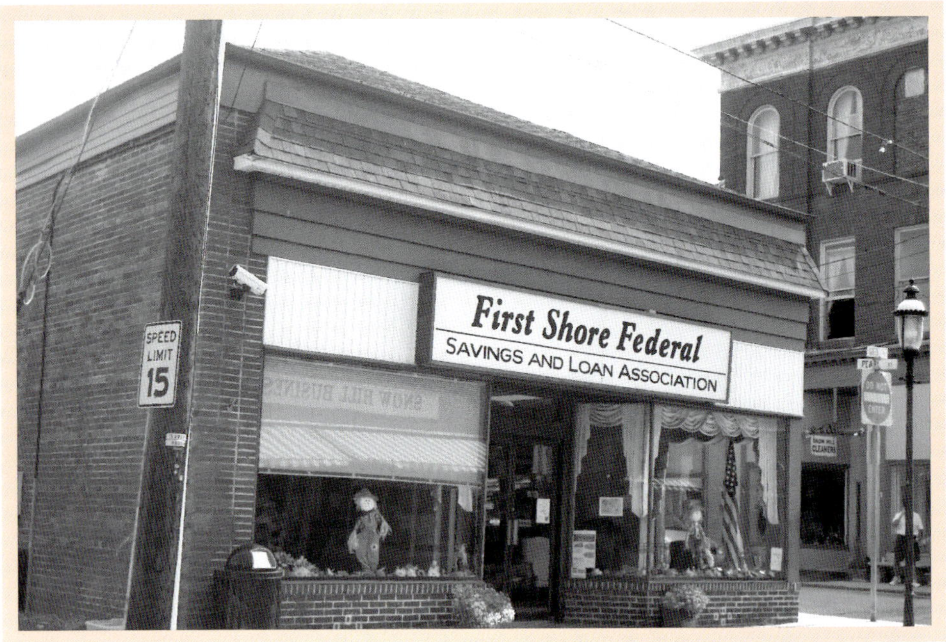

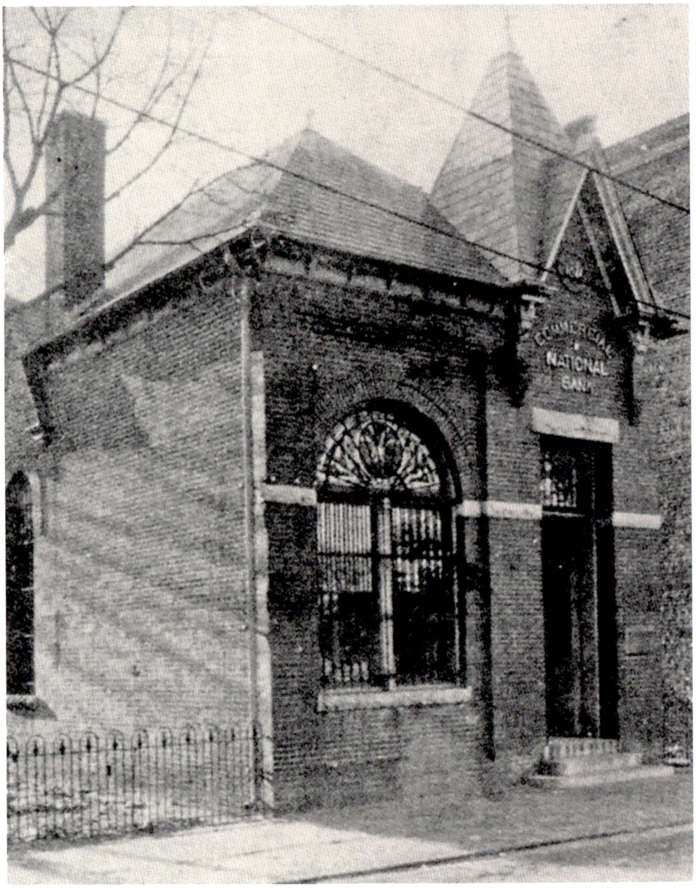

The Commercial National Bank was constructed in 1897. Built of brick with colored-glass windows, the bank stands in the heart of Snow Hill. Later used as the law offices of Hearne and Bailey, the bank was reworked in 1989 by the Worcester County commissioners to provide additional office space. Now the building is occupied by M&T Bank. Little structural work has been done. (Then photograph courtesy of Worcester County Library; now photograph by the author.)

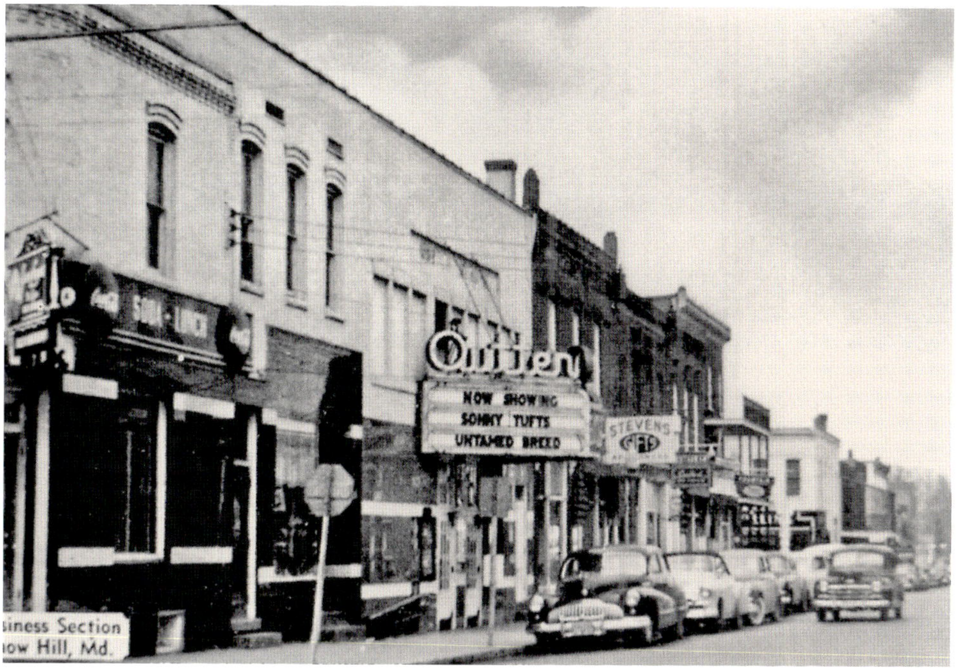

The above picture of the Outten Movie Theater on Washington Street was taken in 1948. It was converted from Mason's Opera House. The movie playing at the time was a Western called *The Untamed Breed*. Now the buildings facing north Washington Street include Curves, a women's workout center; the American art gallery, which is where the theater was once located; and empty store fronts that are available for lease or for sale. (Then photograph courtesy of Worcester County Library; now photograph by the author.)

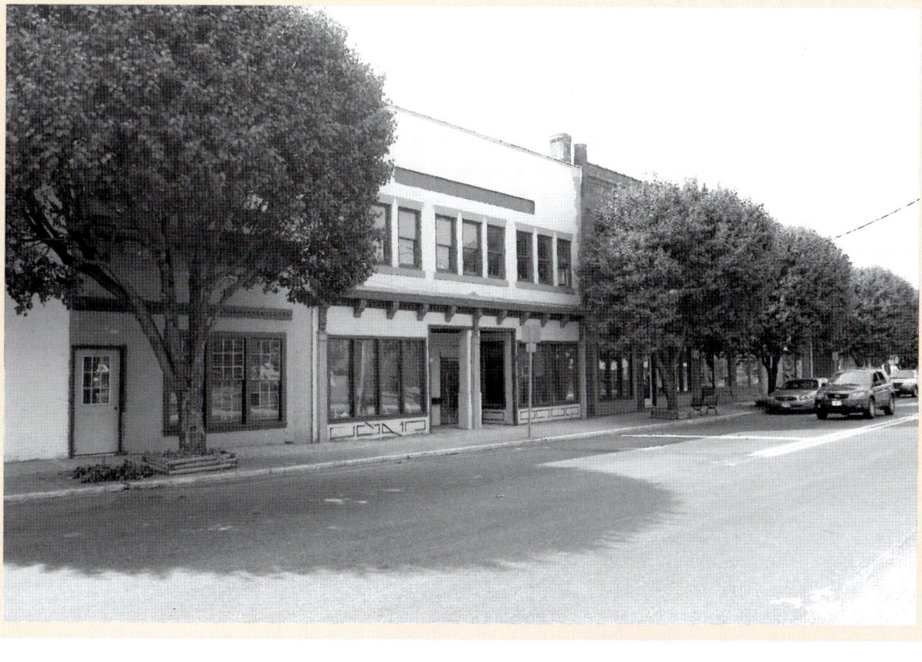

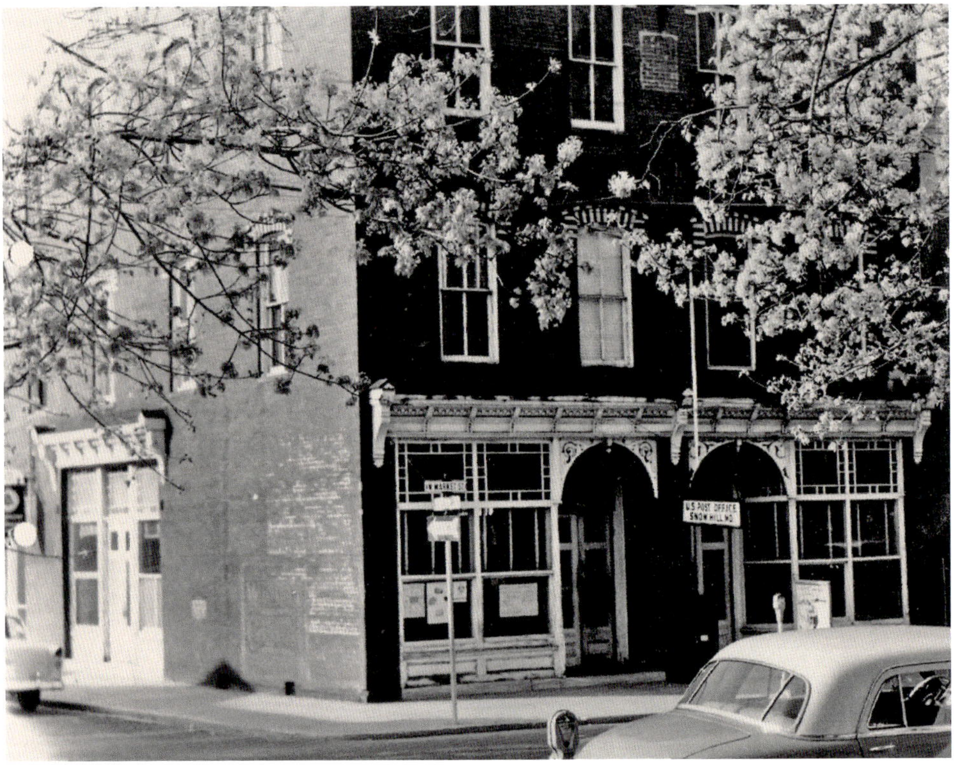

The U.S. Post Office in Snow Hill was placed on the corner of Pearl and Market Streets directly across from the Worcester County Courthouse. It later was moved, and now the post office is on North Washington Street. The building once occupied by the post office is now the Worcester County Tourism building. (Then photograph courtesy of Worcester County Library; now photograph by the author.)

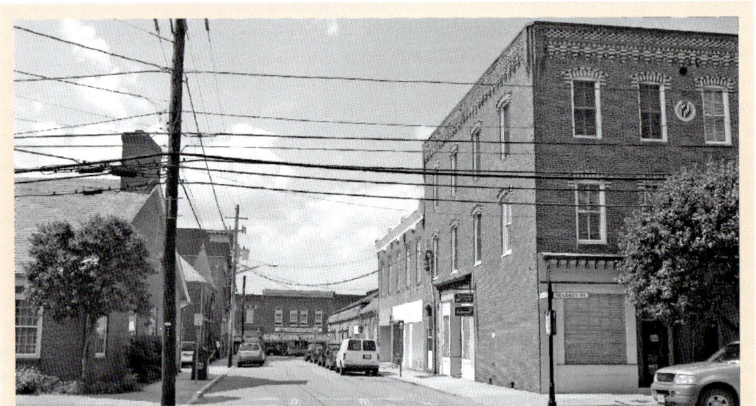

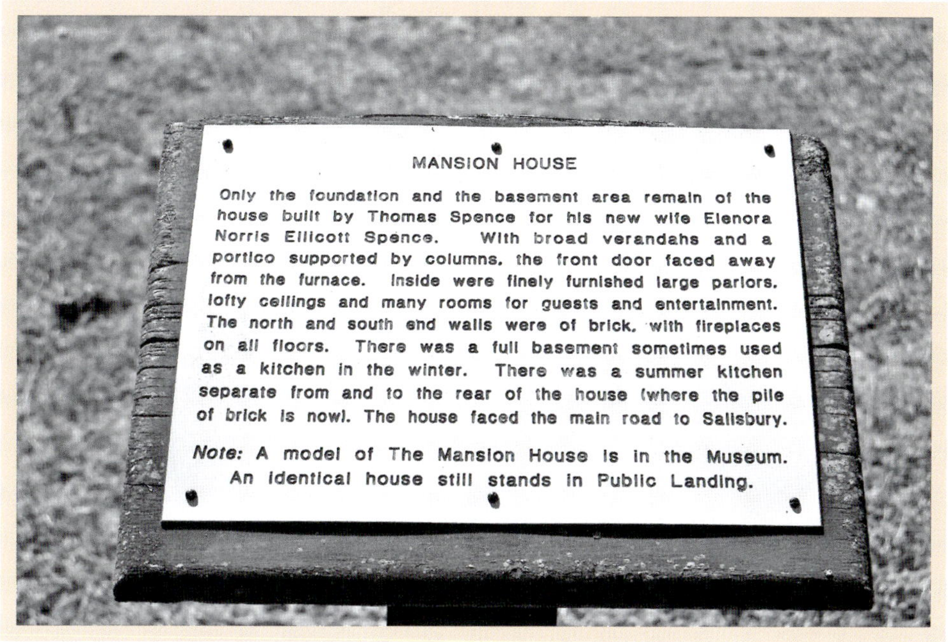

The Mansion House, built around 1830, was located in what is now known as Furnace Town. This was home to iron master George Alfred Townsend. It became a landmark because of the book titled *The Entailed Hat*, which was written by Townsend. The picture below, taken in 1910, shows the house in a state of disrepair. The home is no longer standing. The Mansion House in Public Landing is nearly identical and is still standing. (Then photograph courtesy of Worcester County Library; now photograph by the author.)

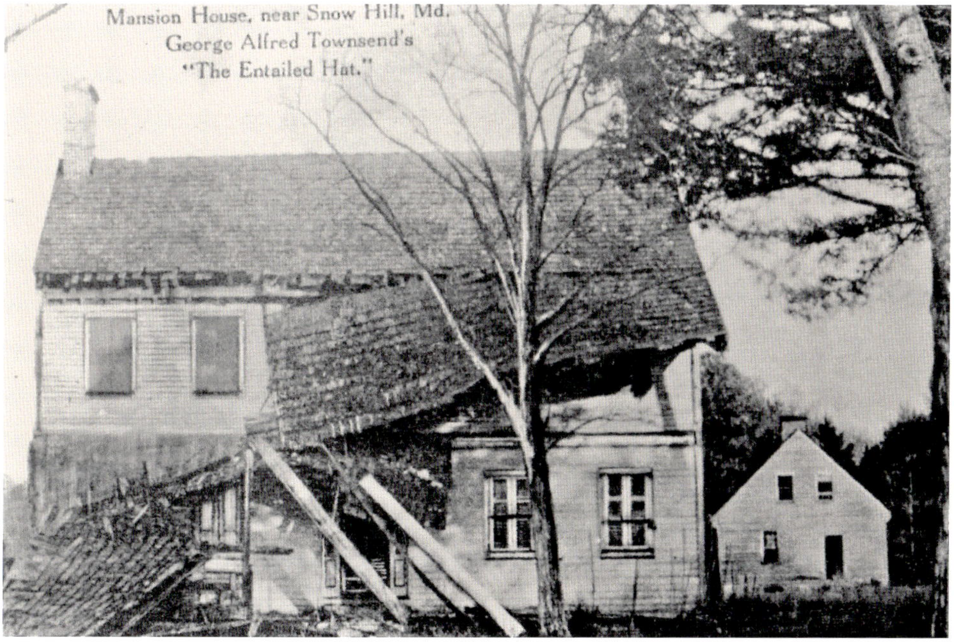

The Nassawango Iron Furnace was built in 1829 and ran until 1847. The purpose of the furnace was to extract or smelt iron from ore. In 1837, Thomas A. Spence took over ownership of the furnace and brought in 700 tons of pig iron per year, making it profitable. However, he was forced to shut down the furnace after only 10 years of production. The expected quantity and quality of the ore was found to be below acceptable standards. In the early 1960s, the owners donated the property to the Worcester County Historical Society. Today Furnace Town is a local tourist attraction known to host fairs and weddings, and for its annual haunted trail during Halloween. (Then photograph courtesy of Worcester County Library; now photograph by the author.)

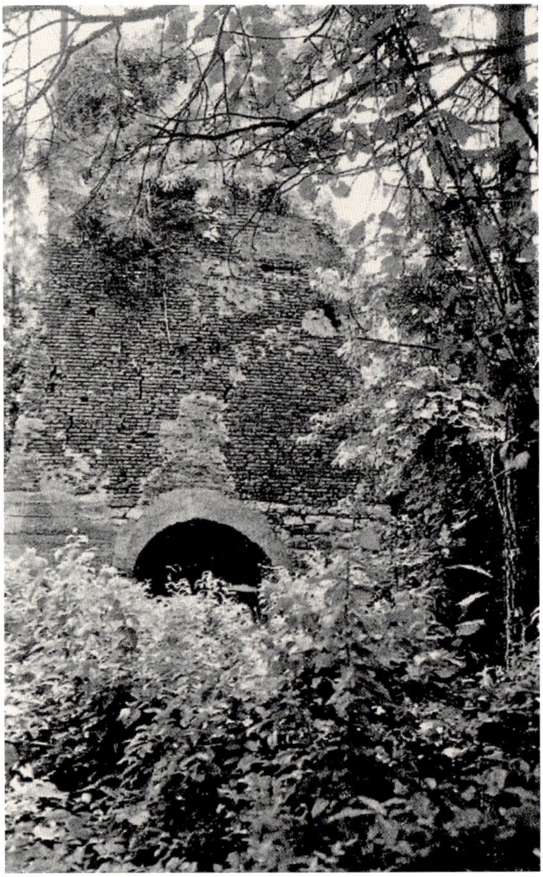

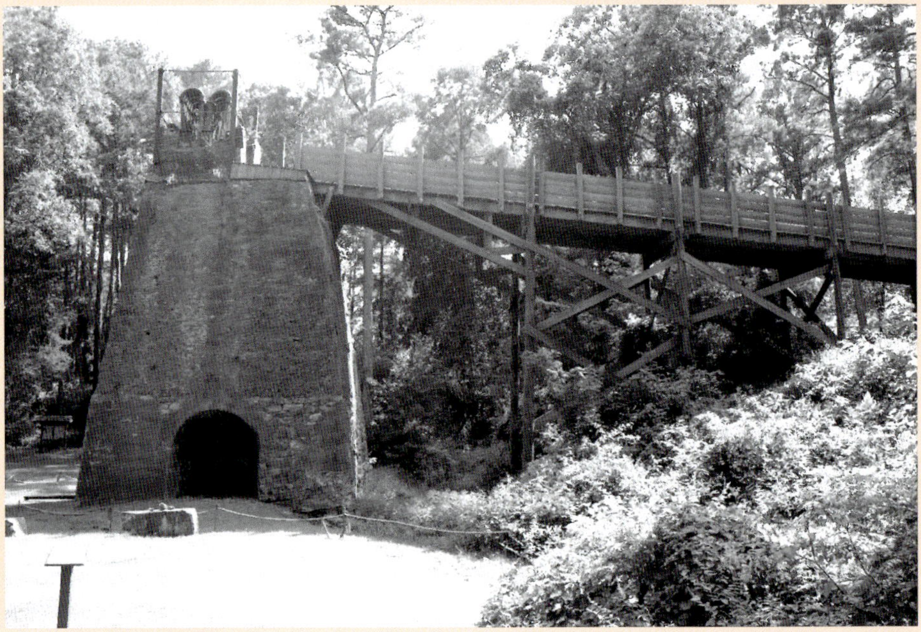

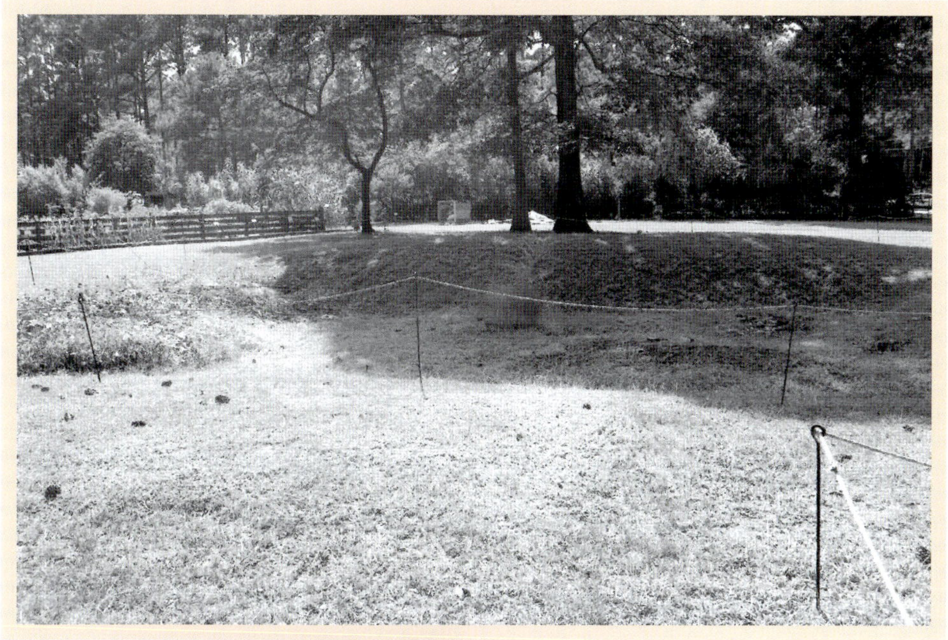

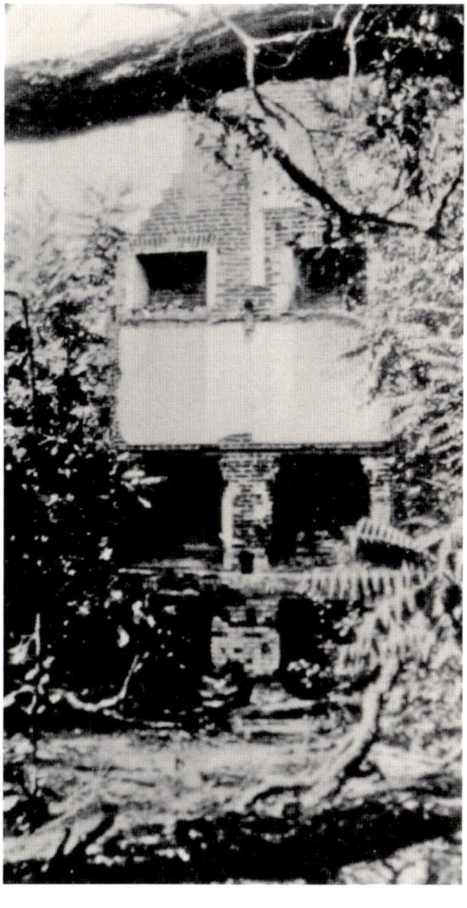

Shown here is all that remains at Furnace Town of George Alfred Townsend's Mansion House. In 1884, Townsend made his house a landmark with his book *The Entailed Hat*. His historical novel romanticized life on the Eastern Shore in the late 19th century. He also wrote *Tales of the Chesapeake* in 1880. Today a rope marks the border of the home's resting place. (Then photograph courtesy of Worcester County Library; now photograph by the author.)

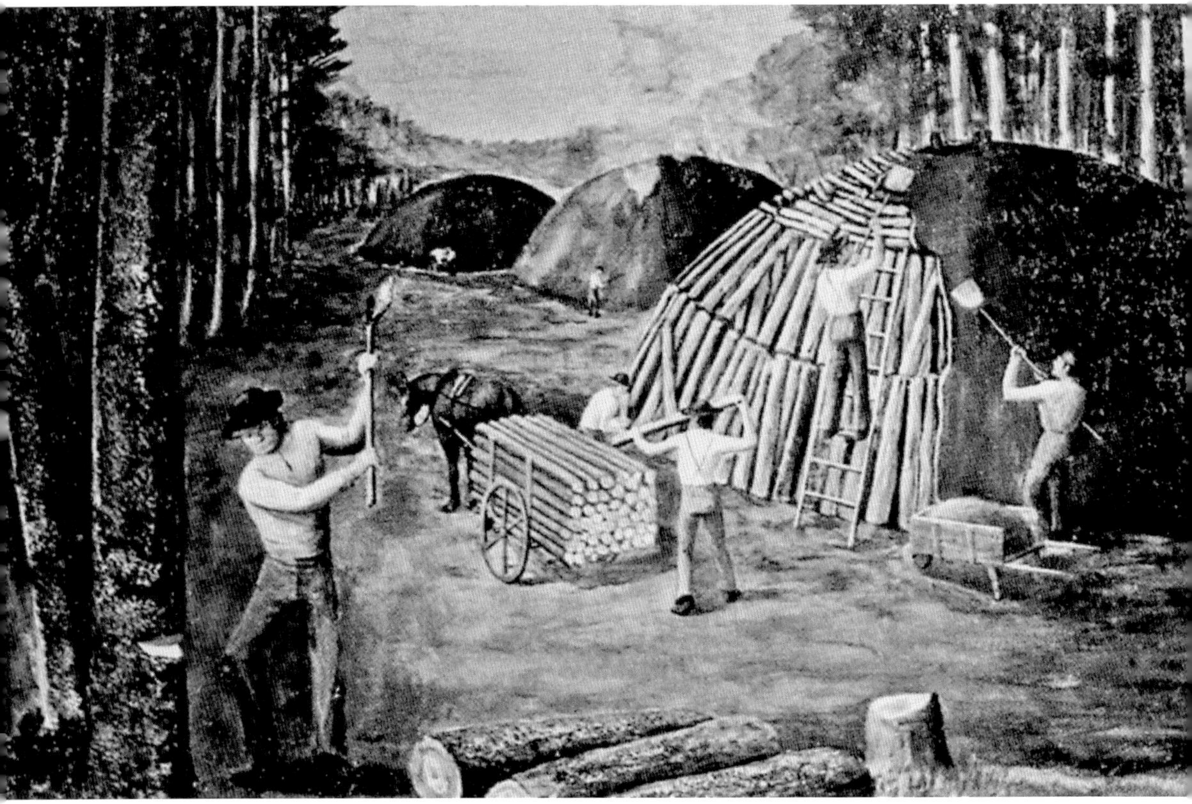

This postcard has been reprinted many times. Its original print date is unknown but is thought to be some time in the 1930s. Today the postcard is in color and can be found at Furnace Town in the gift shop. The postcard depicts the workmen of Furnace Town. (Then photograph courtesy of Worcester County Library; now photograph by the author.)

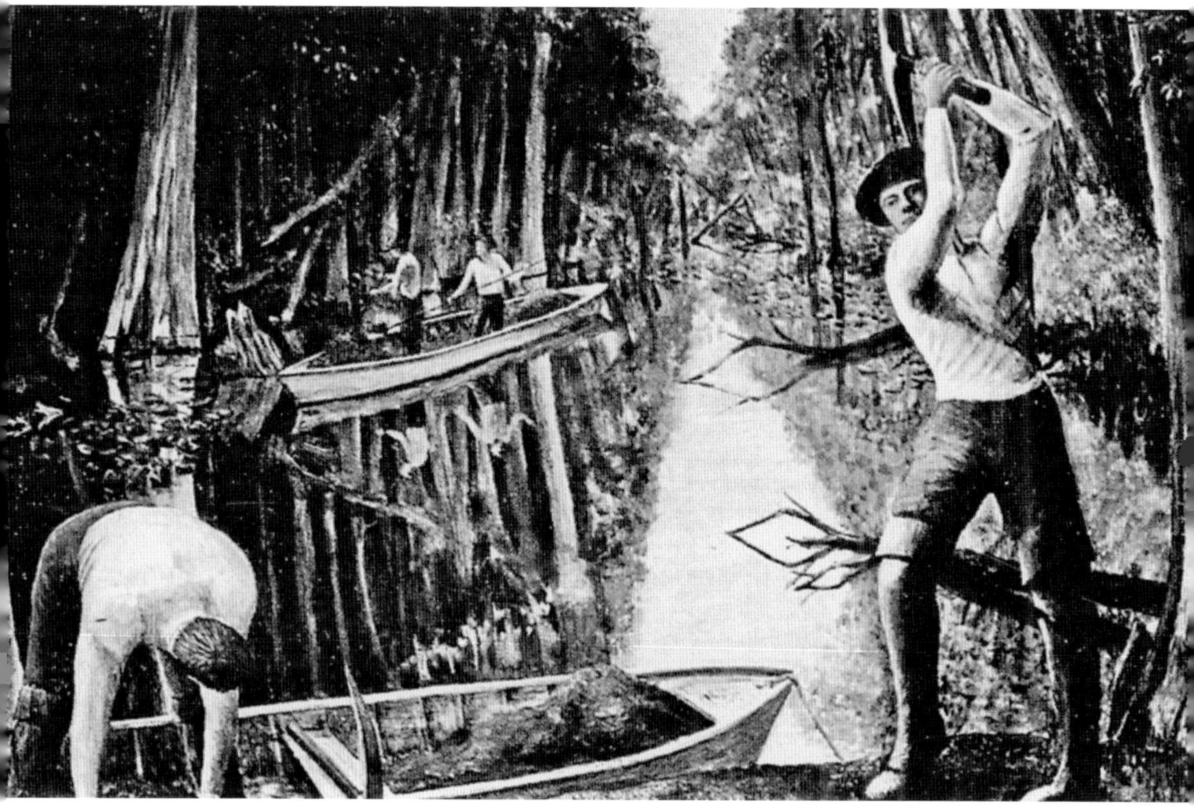

Seen here is a postcard from Furnace Town. Again, its original print date is unknown, but it is said to be from the 1930s. This postcard, today produced in color, can also be bought at Furnace Town in the gift shop and at Pusey's Country Store on Route 12. (Then photograph courtesy of Worcester County Library; now photograph by the author.)

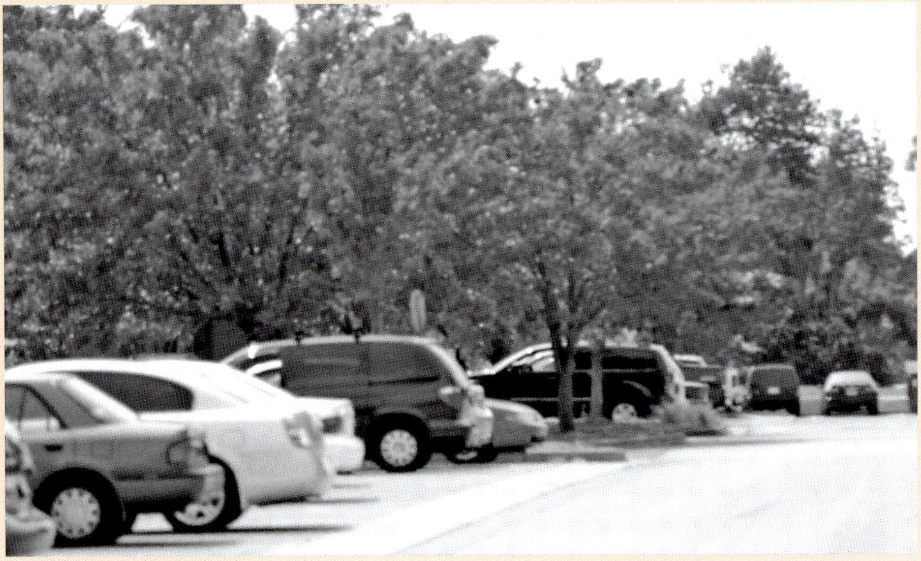

The C. E. Chandler sawmill was in Snow Hill prior to 1923 but not before 1911, per dated maps. The business was owned by C. E. Chandler and was located on the banks of the Pocomoke River. Today the social service parking lot is in its place. (Then photograph courtesy of Worcester County Library; now photograph by the author.)

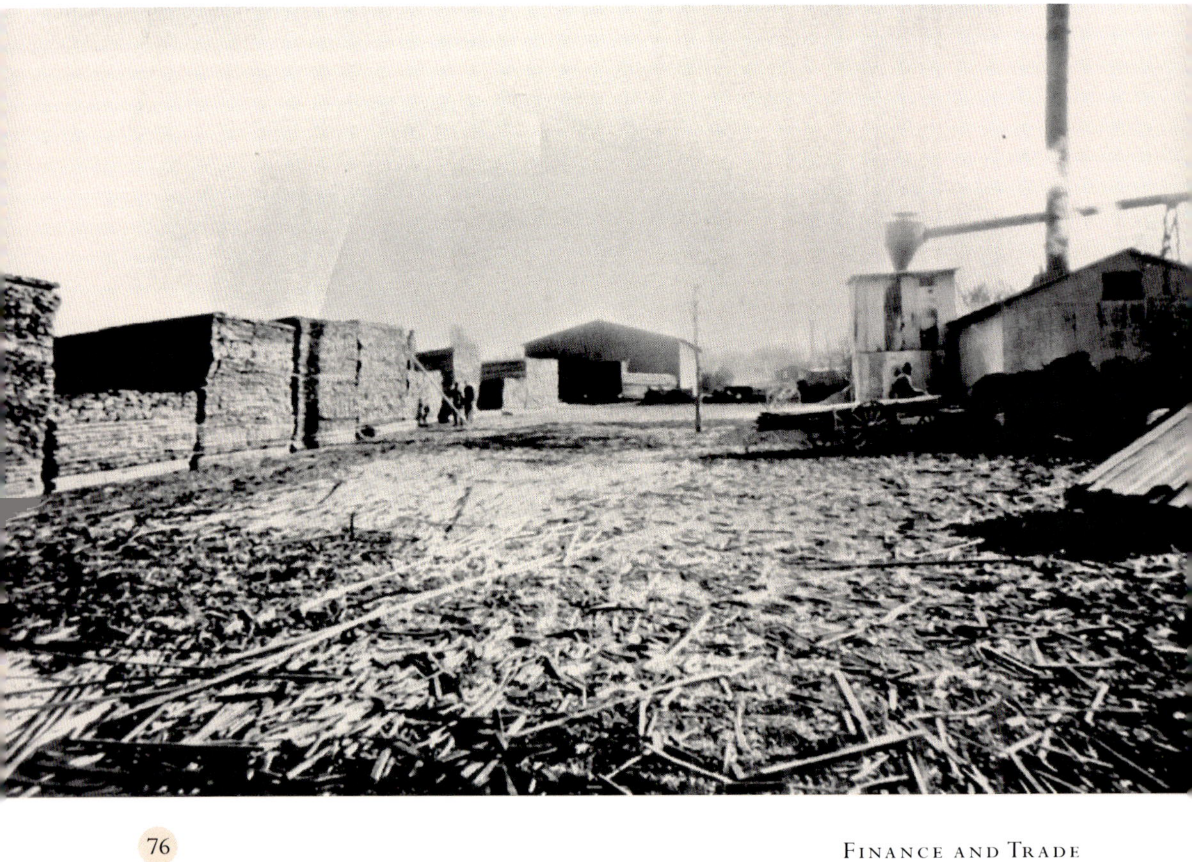

CHAPTER 6

COMMUNITY OF BELIEF

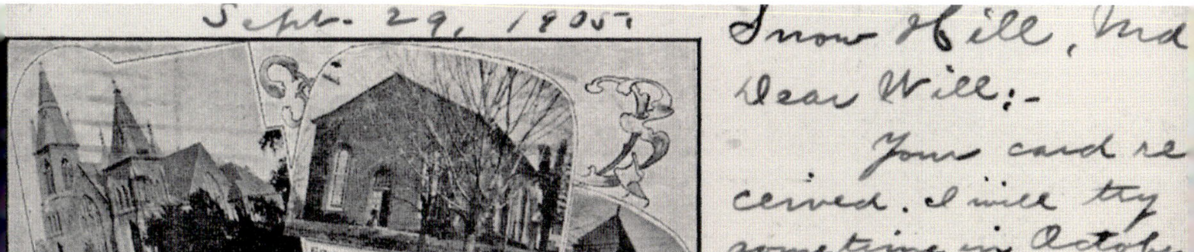

This postcard, dated 1905, was in the collection at the Worchester County Library. It is among the oldest legible postcards. It was written to a "Will," possibly William Purnell of Snow Hilll, and was signed by Ellen Herne. The front of the card shows a collection of the towns religious dwellings. (Then photograph courtesy of Worcester County Library.)

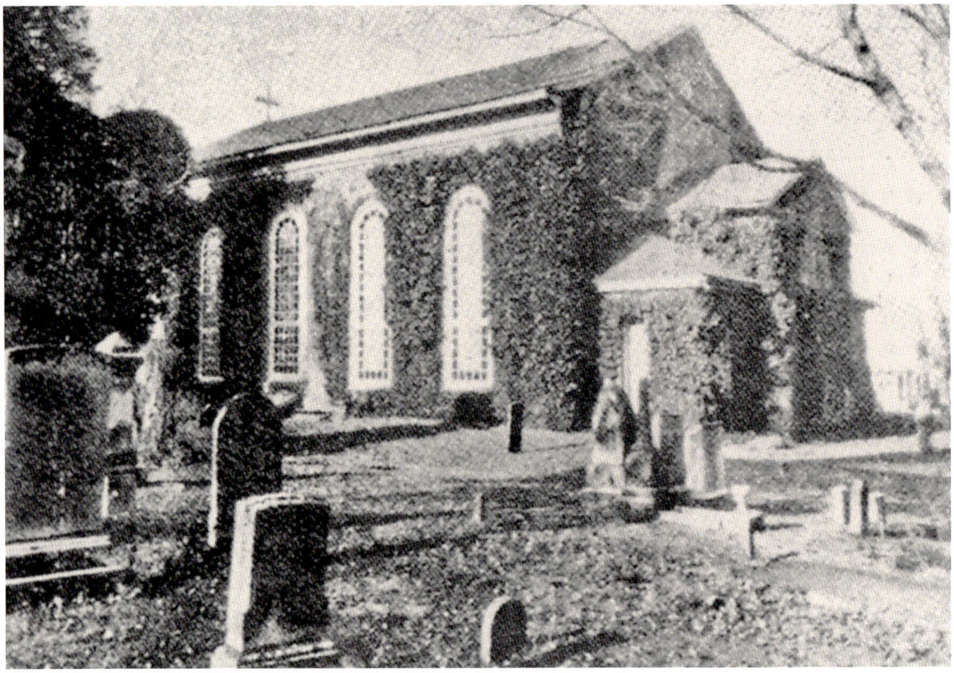

Found on the corner of Market and Church Streets is All Hallows Episcopal Church. Built in 1756, All Hallows was at the time the most expensive Anglican church built on the Eastern Shore. In 1748, the Maryland General Assembly authorized a levy of 80,000 pounds to fund construction. The cost to finish the church went over the initial budget, and an additional 45,000 pounds was levied to finish the building. (Then photograph courtesy of Worcester County Library; now photograph by the author.)

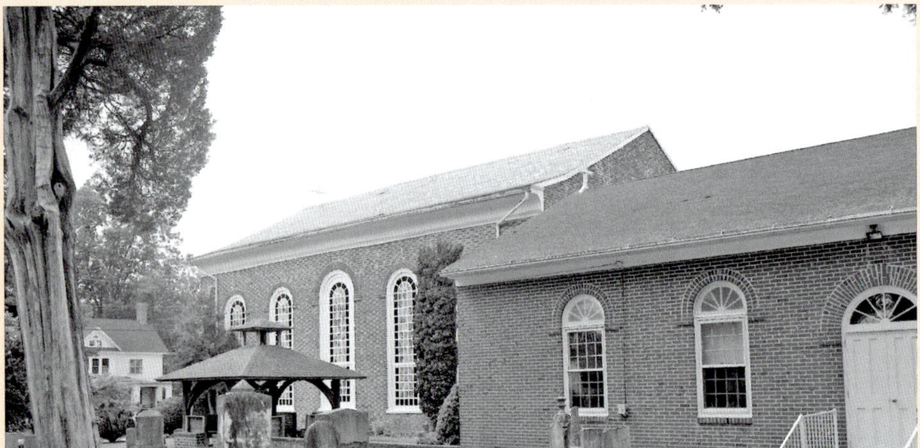

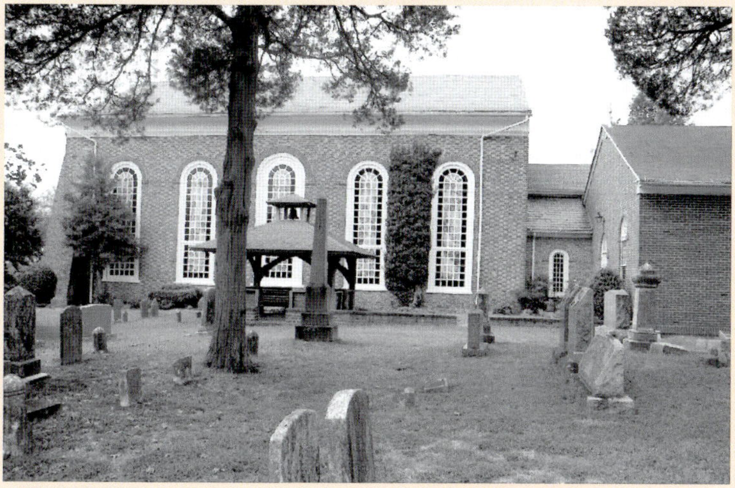

The documents for the construction of All Hallows Episcopal Church were destroyed in the fire of 1834. It took eight years to build under the supervision of Rev. Patrick Glasgow. The church remained unaltered for 18 years, until the east end was remodeled. In 1956, a parish hall was added that extends eastward. The church has rendered an addition as well as updates since. The current father is Kenneth Thom. All Hollows Episcopal Church still hosts services every Sunday followed by a social hour for all attending to enjoy homemade dishes and discussions. (Then photograph courtesy of Worcester County Library; now photograph by the author.)

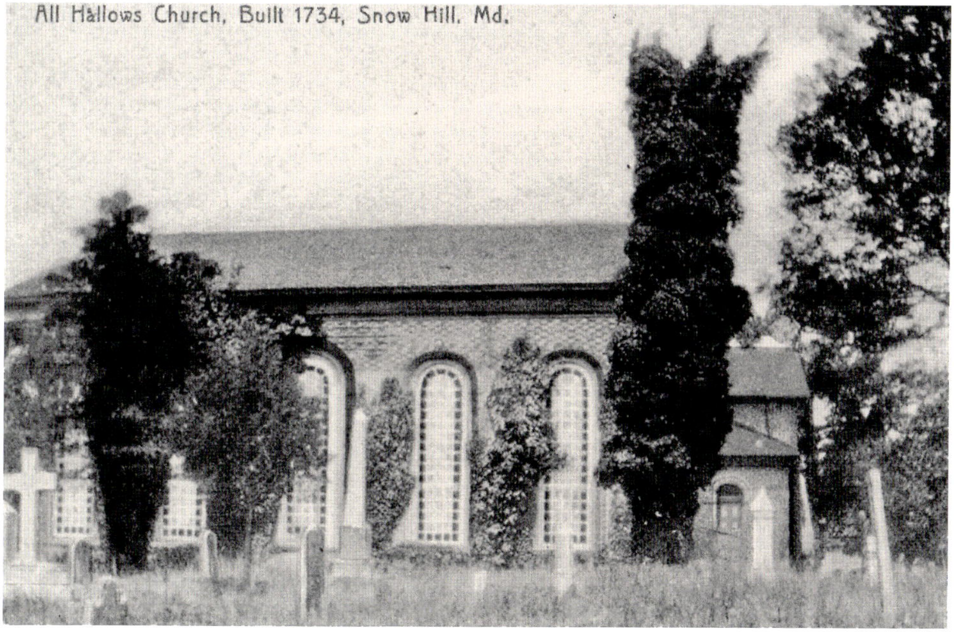

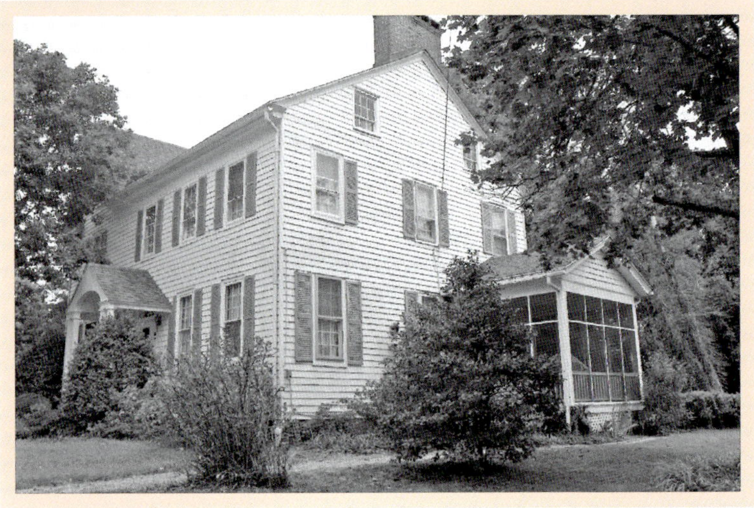

The All Hallows Episcopal Church rectory was constructed during the 1820s. This two-story house sits on the south side of West Federal Street. It was built on two lots purchased by Thomas T. Dorman in August 1809 for $250. After his death in 1832, his widow, Susannah, married Littleton Devereux. They lived in the house for the next 12 years until she gave the house to the vestry of All Hallows Parish for its future use. It has remained in the possession of the church since 1843. (Then photograph courtesy of Worcester County Library; now photograph by the author.)

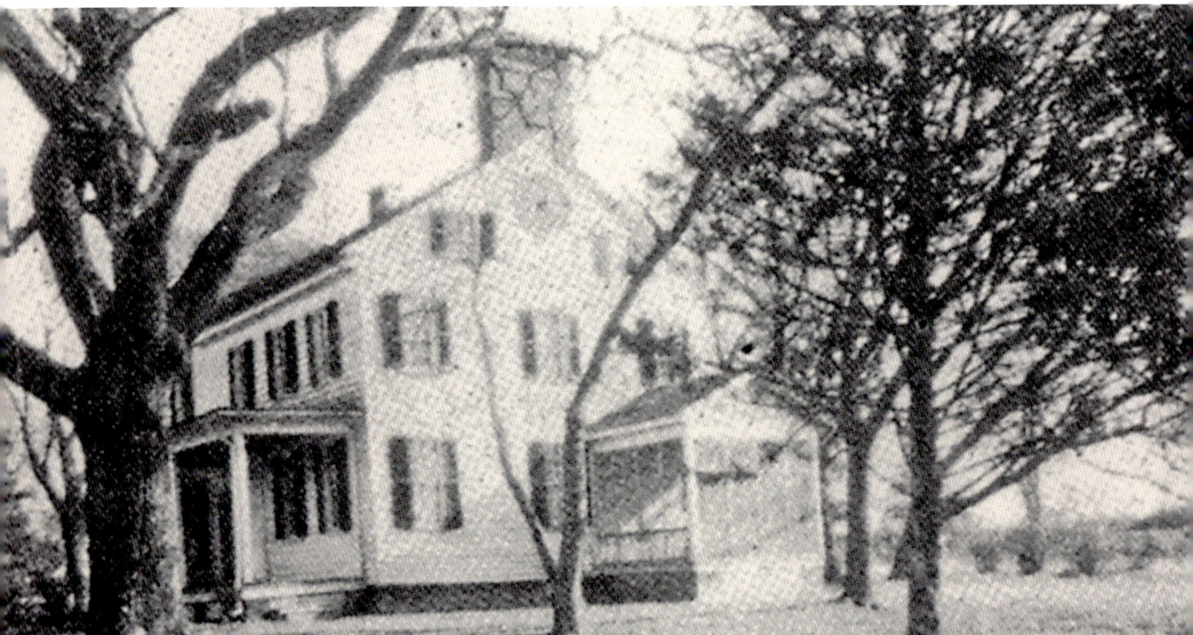

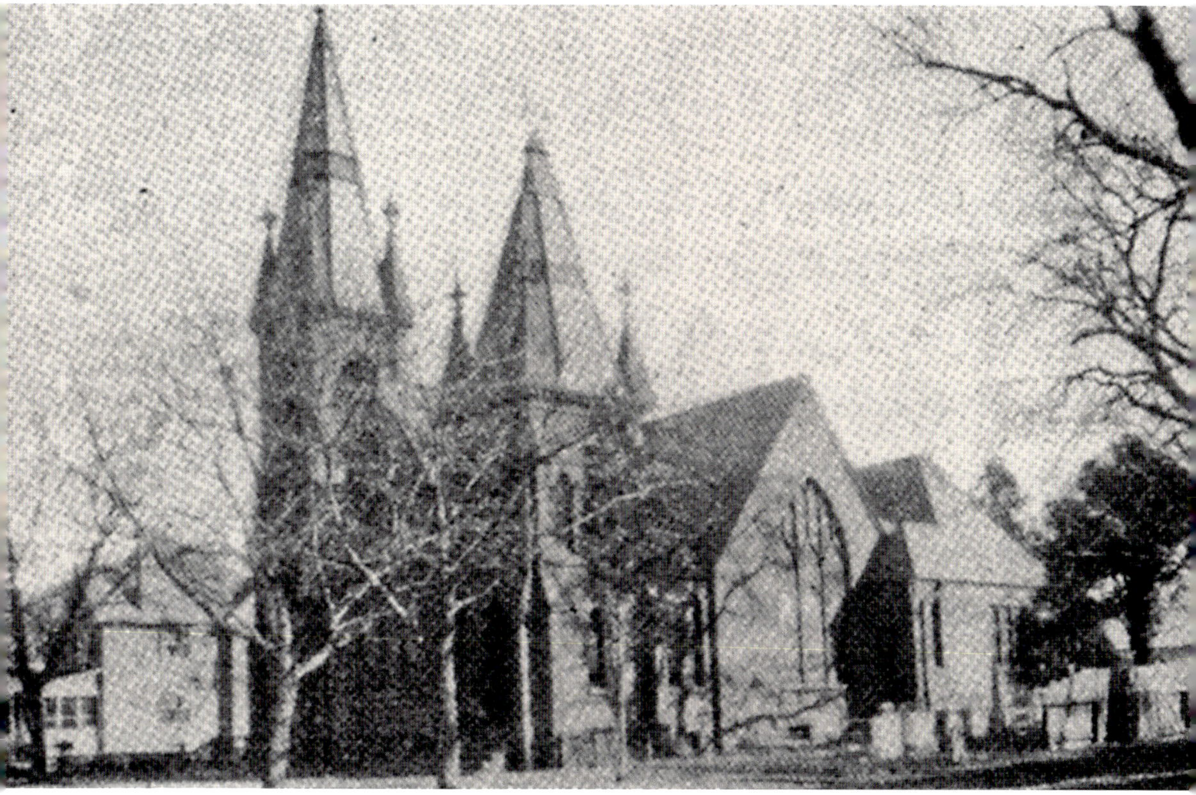

Makemie Memorial Presbyterian Church was dedicated in 1888 and is the only church in Worcester County to be built in the Gothic Revival style. Due to an extensive collection of papers, including daybooks, receipts, lists of materials, and freight costs, there is thorough documentation of its construction. Francis Makemie, for whom the church is named, organized early Presbyterian meetings from Snow Hill to Accomack County, Virginia. The church still provides a service on Sundays. (Then photograph courtesy of Worcester County Library; now photograph by the author.)

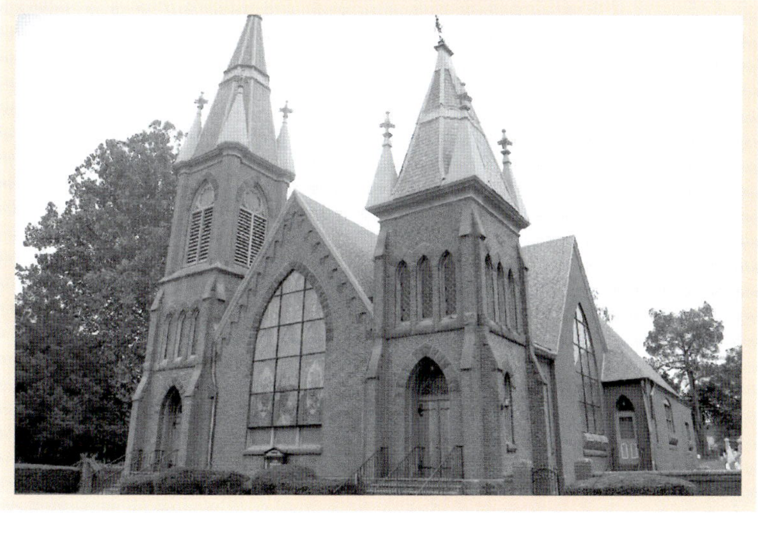

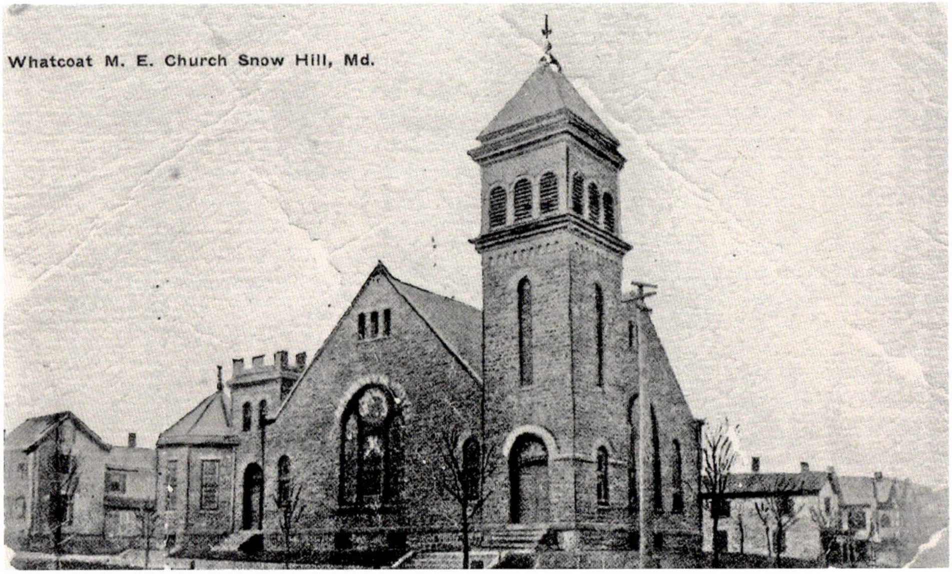

Standing on the corner of South Washington and West Federal Streets is Whatcoat Methodist Episcopal Church. This three-story church was built on October 7, 1899, and was named for Rev. Richard Whatcoat. No alterations have been made to the church except for a Sunday school addition on the north side of the building during the 1950s. The original church has been untouched and is a beautiful sight. During the first weekend of the month, the church holds an indoor opportunity shop. (Then photograph courtesy of Worcester County Library; now photograph by the author.)

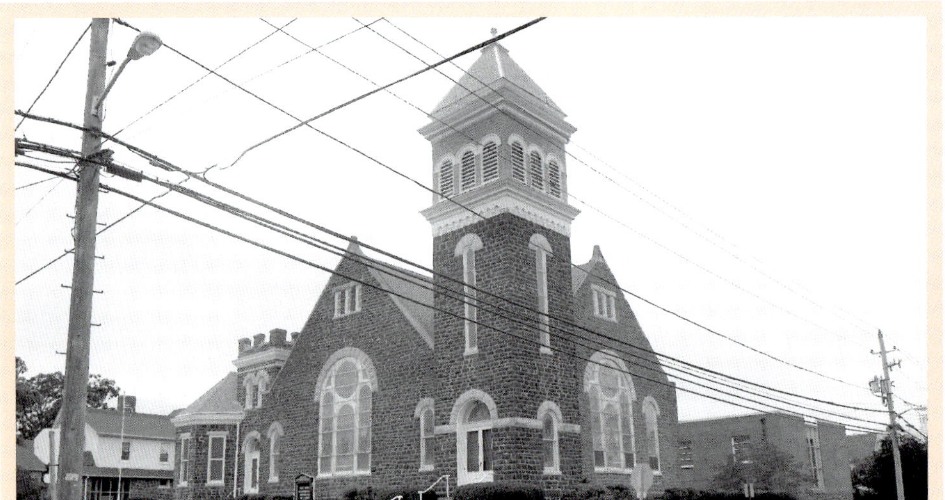

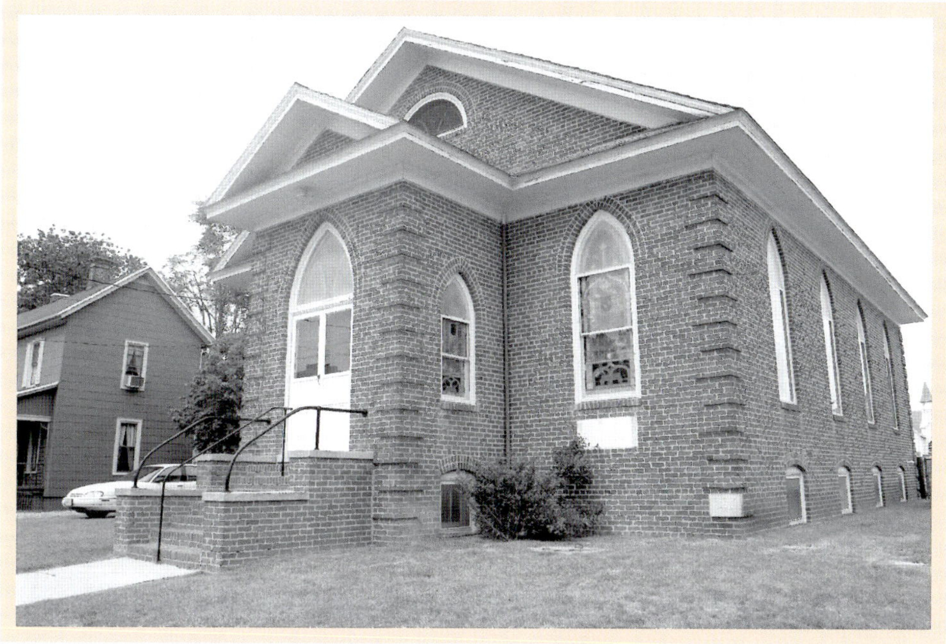

The Old School Baptist Church was established in 1876. The building originally housed the Whatcoat Methodist Church in the early 19th century. This single-story brick structure was once made of wood. It was moved from its original site on East Federal Street sometime before the Snow Hill map of 1877. In 1924, the wooden church was replaced by this brick structure. Today it continues to hold weekly worship services on Sundays. (Then photograph courtesy of Worcester County Library; now photograph by the author.)

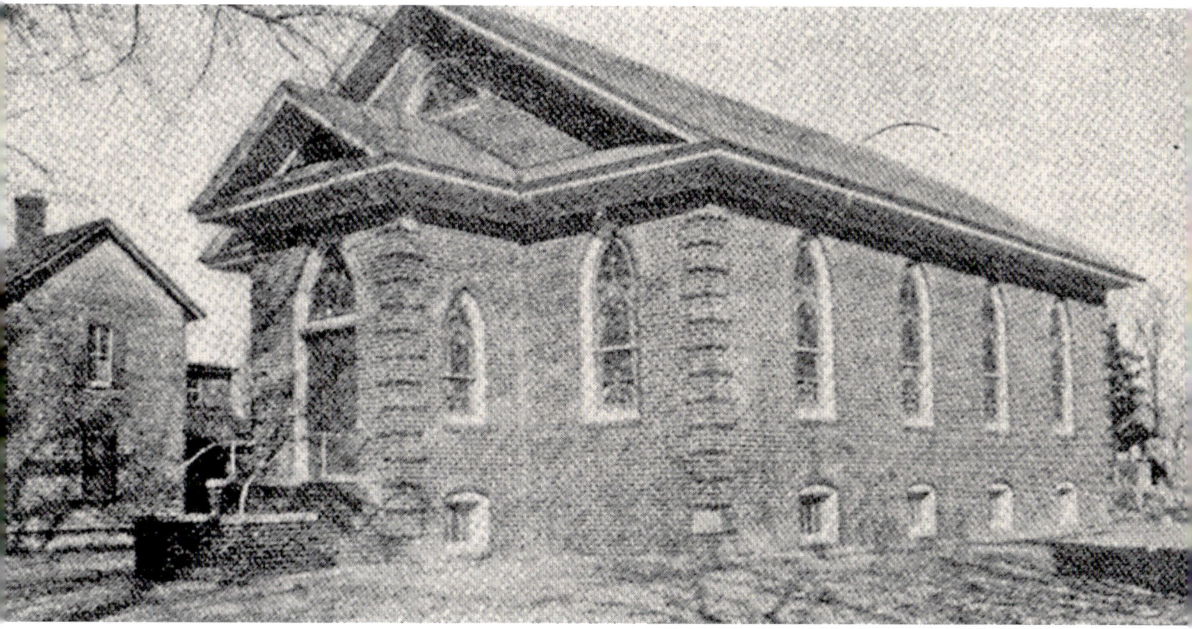

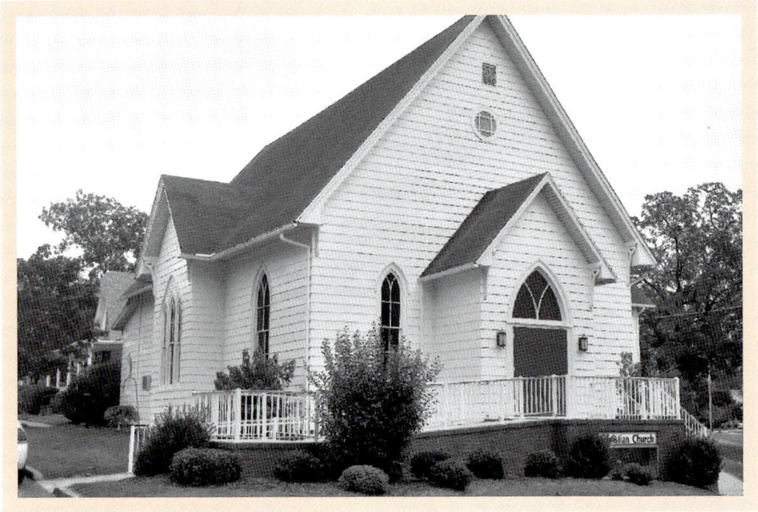

Old School Baptist Church was established in 1876 and originally housed the Whatcoat Methodist Church in the early 19th century. This single-story brick building was once a shingled wood church and was moved from its original site on East Federal Street some time before the Snow Hill atlas map of 1877. The church remained in its original condition until 1924, when this brick structure replaced the old one. The church is still in service. (Then photograph courtesy of the Worcester County Library; now photograph by the author.)

CHAPTER 7

From the Ground Up

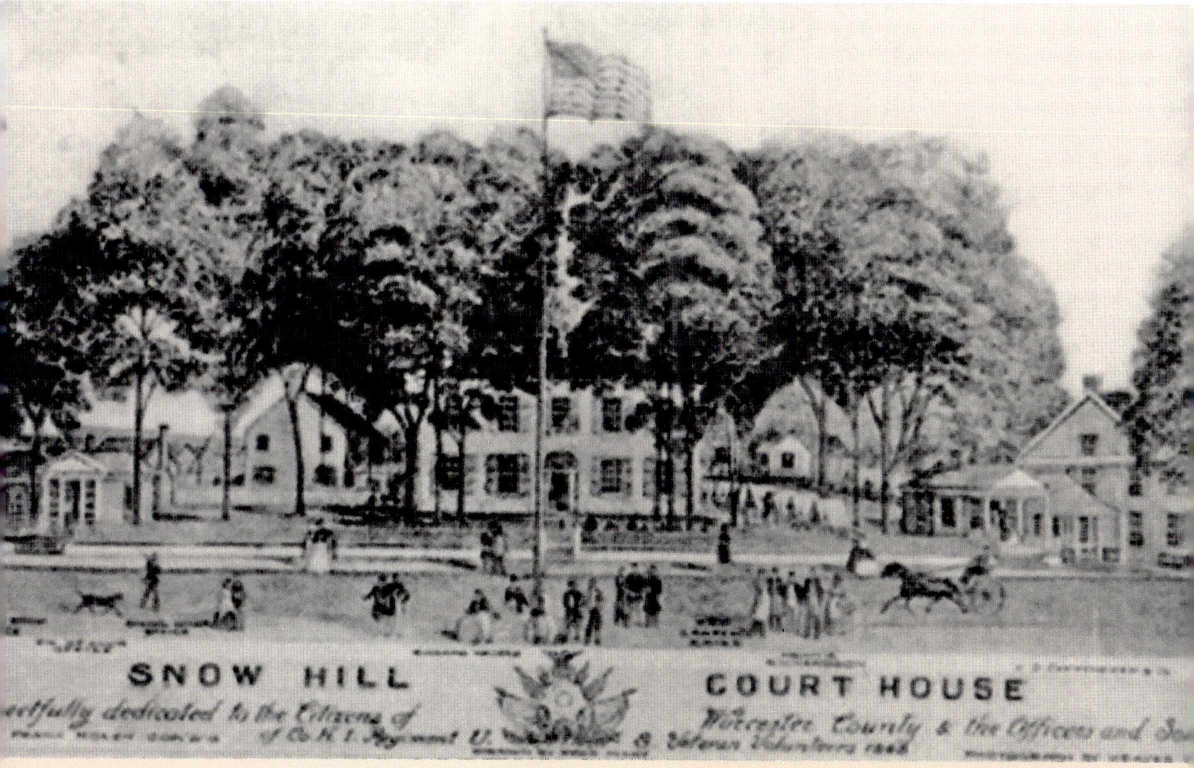

The Worcester County Courthouse was destroyed by fire in 1893; it was the second courthouse consumed by flames. In both cases, valuable early records were lost, as well as history. The courthouse was thought to be secure, so many people brought their valuables to it in order to save them from the fire that had started two blocks away. The estimated loss was $300,000, although it was generally thought to be half a million dollars. Today the courthouse employs more than 200 people and houses many offices, including the Worcester County Sheriff's Department, Worcester County 911, environmental services, the treasurer's office, the circuit court, and the justice of the peace. (Courtesy of Worcester County Library, photograph by the author.)

The Mansion House in Public Landing is shown in disarray after the storm of 1933. Overlooking the Chincoteague Bay, this home changed owners nine times before the surrounding cabins were built up around it. The Mansion House and the surrounding cabins were used as a hotel for entertainment seekers. The Mansion House is now run as a bed-and-breakfast. (Then photograph courtesy of the Worcester County Library; now photograph by the author.)

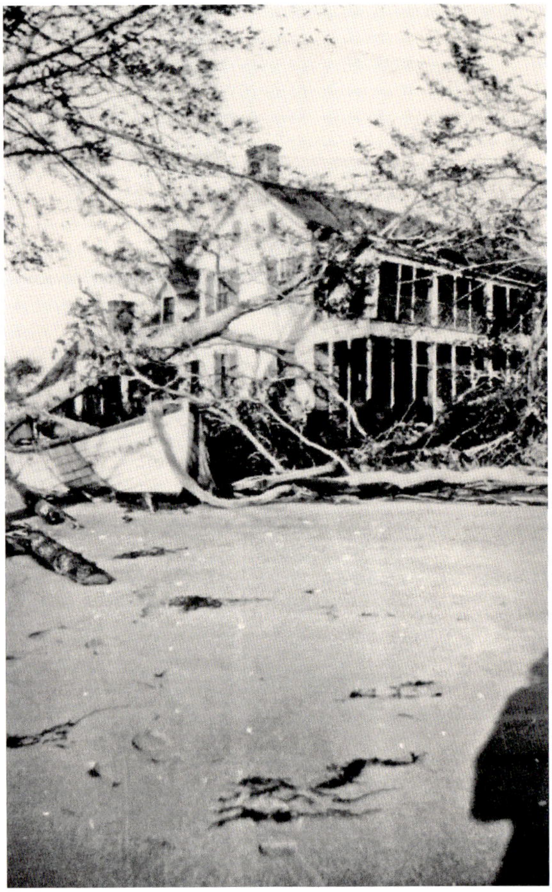

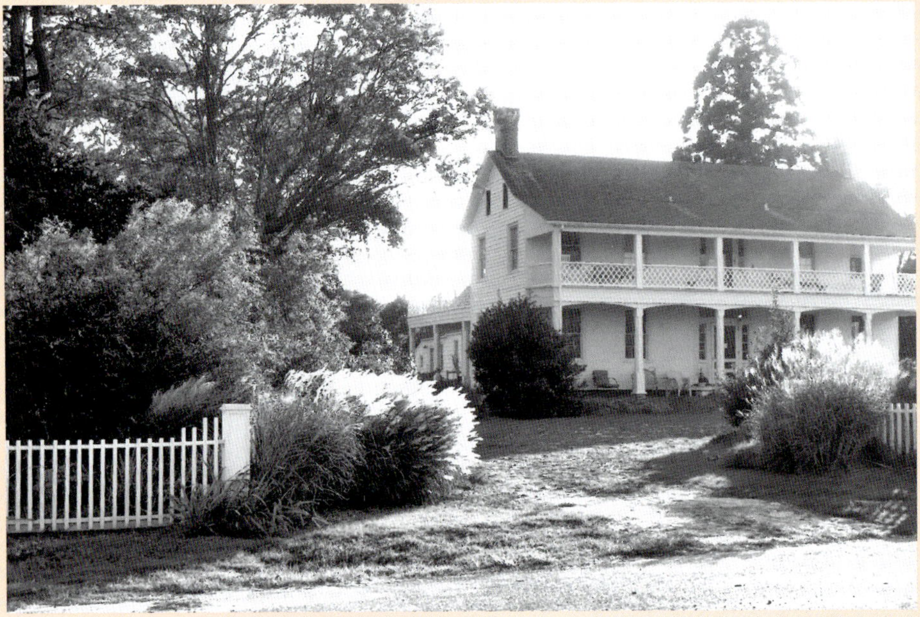

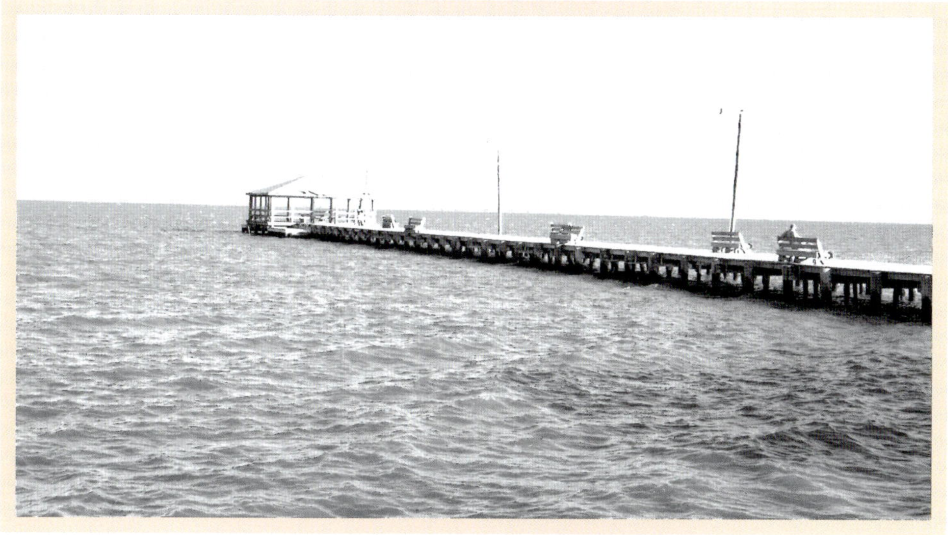

Public Landing is a popular spot for crabbing, fishing, swimming, or just relaxing by the Chincoteague Bay. Prior to 1926, there was just a pier. Construction on Public Landing included a bowling alley, a theater, amusement rides, a sliding board, and a soda shop owned and operated by the Purnell family. The storm of 1933 came up the Chincoteague Bay and destroyed the pier. Today the pier is much like its original construction, but it has been updated with a pavilion at the end. (Then photograph courtesy of the Worcester County Library; now photograph by the author.)

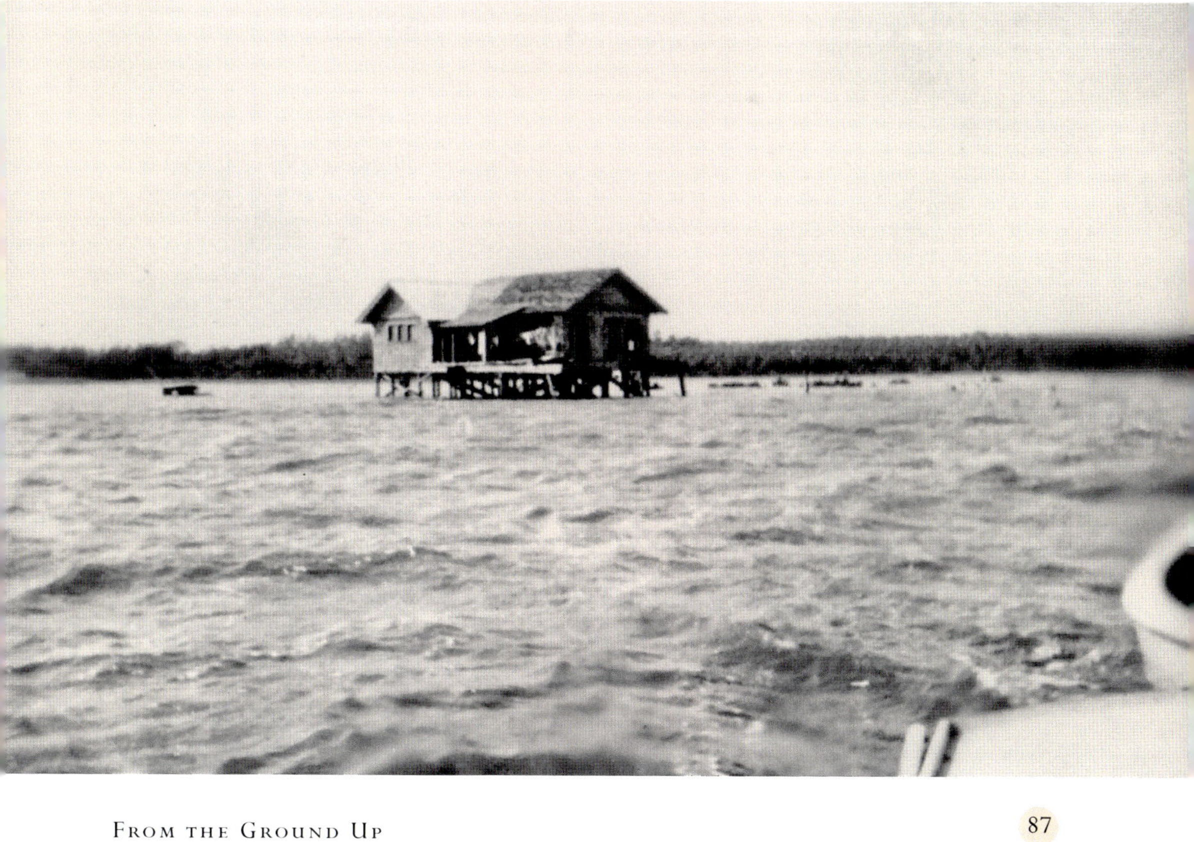

The photograph at right, dated August 26, 1933, is of the aftermath of Hurricane Lulu, or the Chincoteague Potomac Hurricane, which is better known as the Storm of '33. As seen, the storm wiped out most of Public Landing, and the large parking lot was filled with debris from fallen structures. Today the parking lot is still there, and the pier has been rebuilt. (Then photograph courtesy of the Worcester County Library; now photograph by the author.)

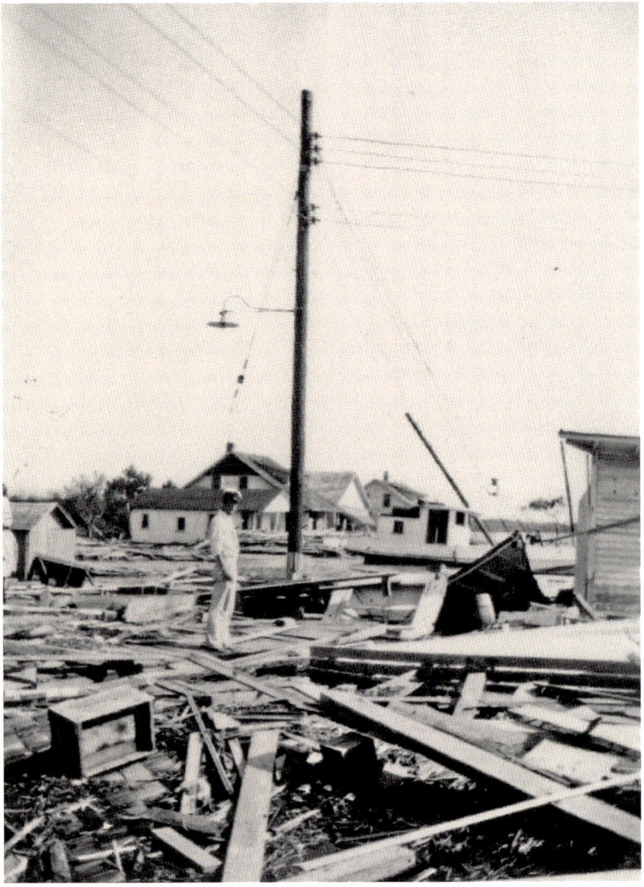

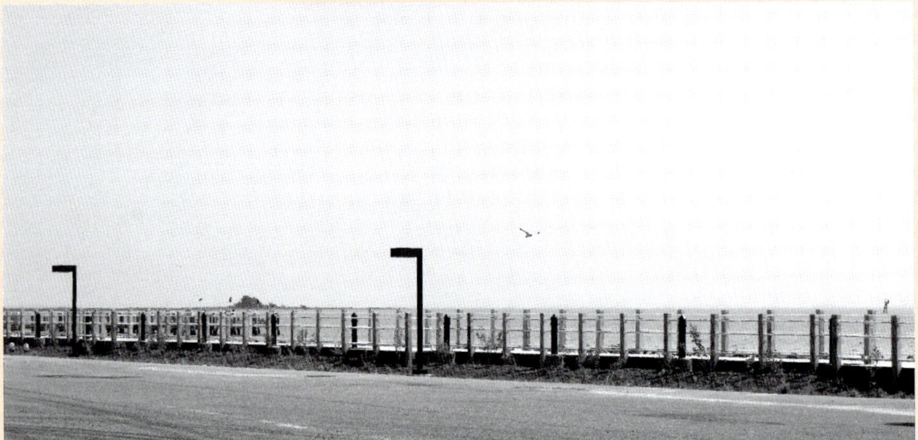

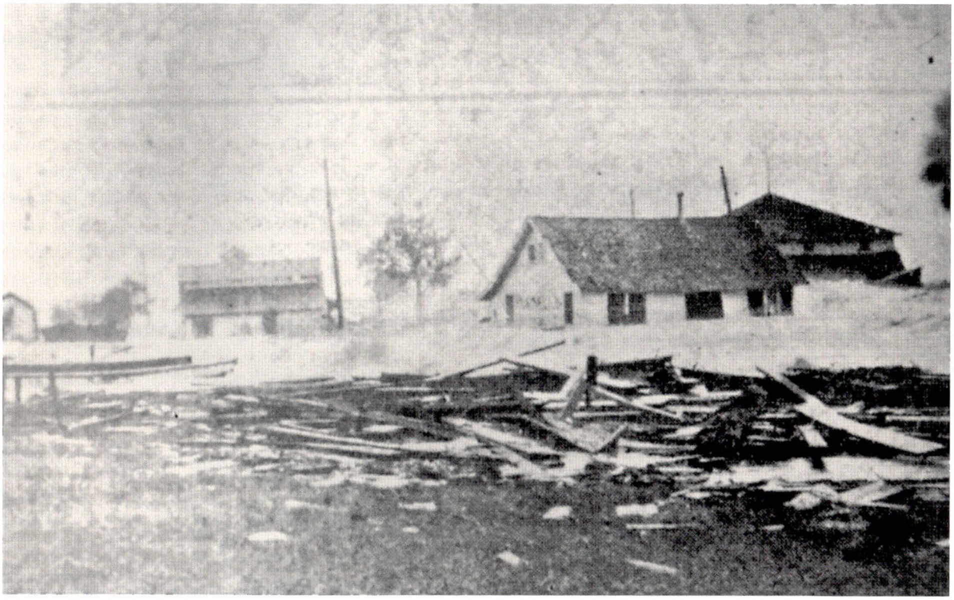

In the photograph above, taken from the pier of Public Landing, Purnell's soda shop is seen in the distance, along with some of what was there before the 1933 storm. Purnell's sold soda, food, gifts, and take-homes about or featuring Public Landing. Entertainment seekers came from all around to visit Public Landing. Today Public Landing is a pier and parking lot. (Then photograph courtesy of Worcester County Library; now photograph by the author.)

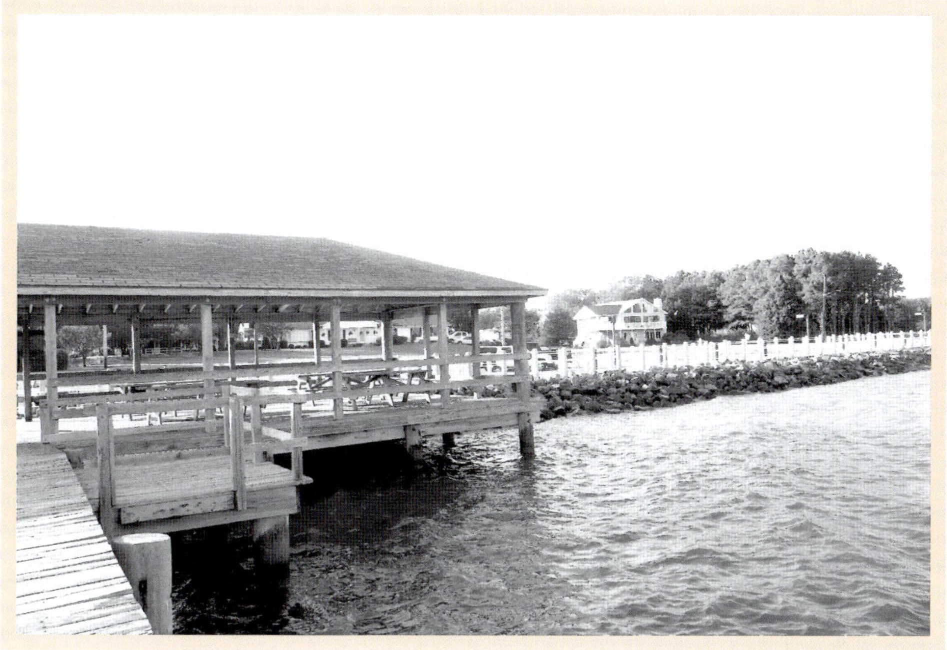

There were many repercussions from the storm of 1933, and flooding was a major player. These homes have been damaged by the storm's flooding. The flood was said to have been up to 5 feet deep in some places. None of the houses exist today. (Then photograph courtesy of Worcester County Library; now photograph by the author.)

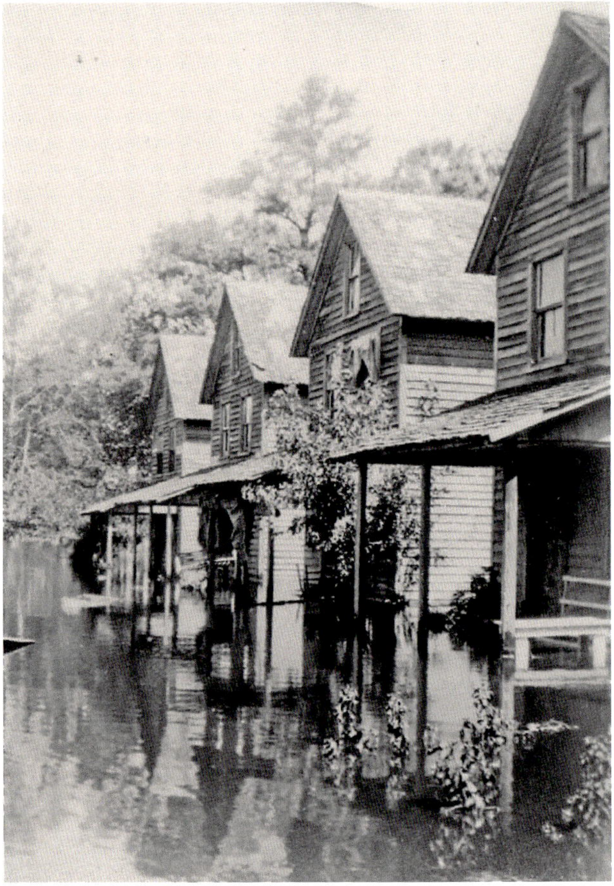

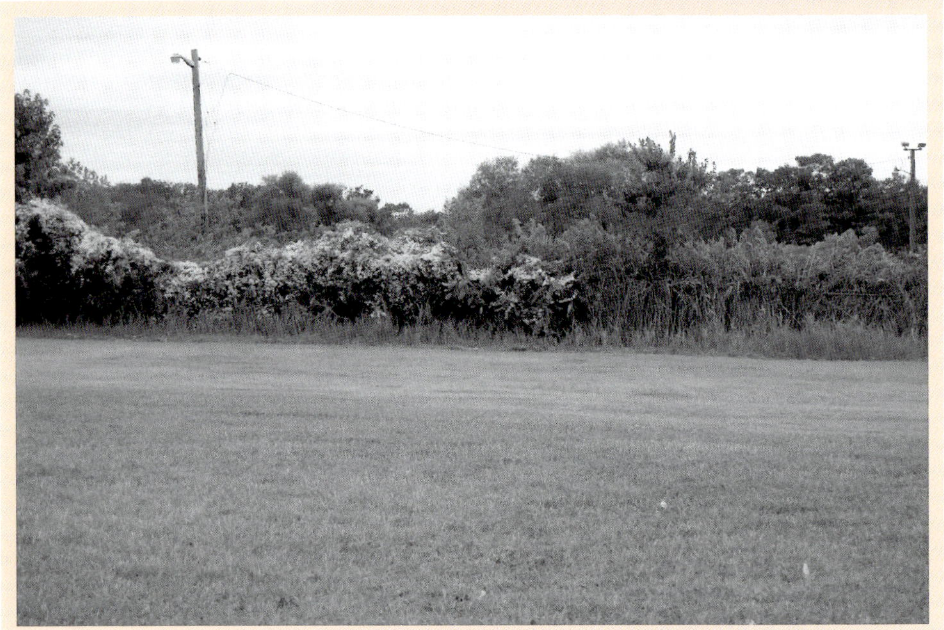

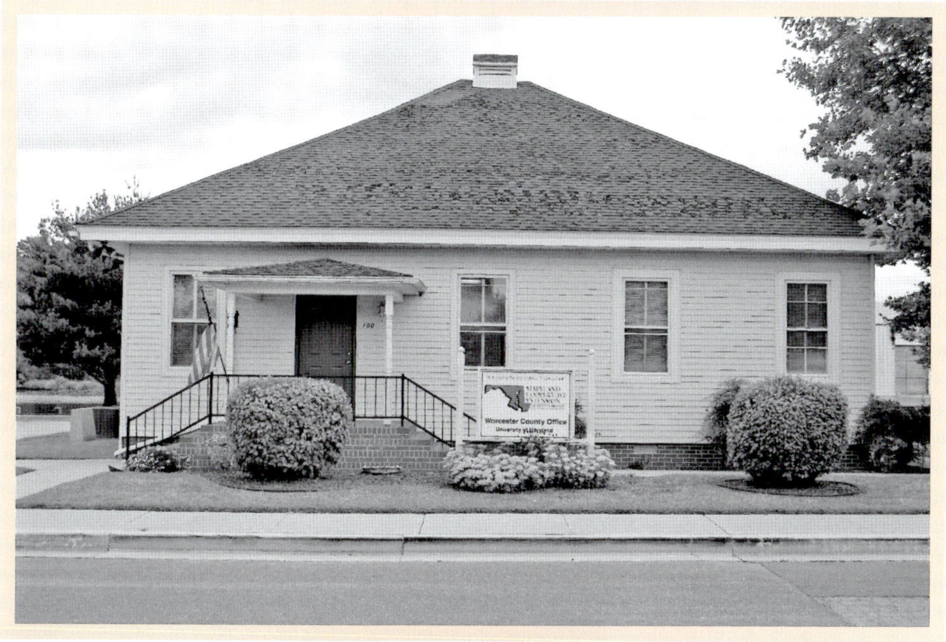

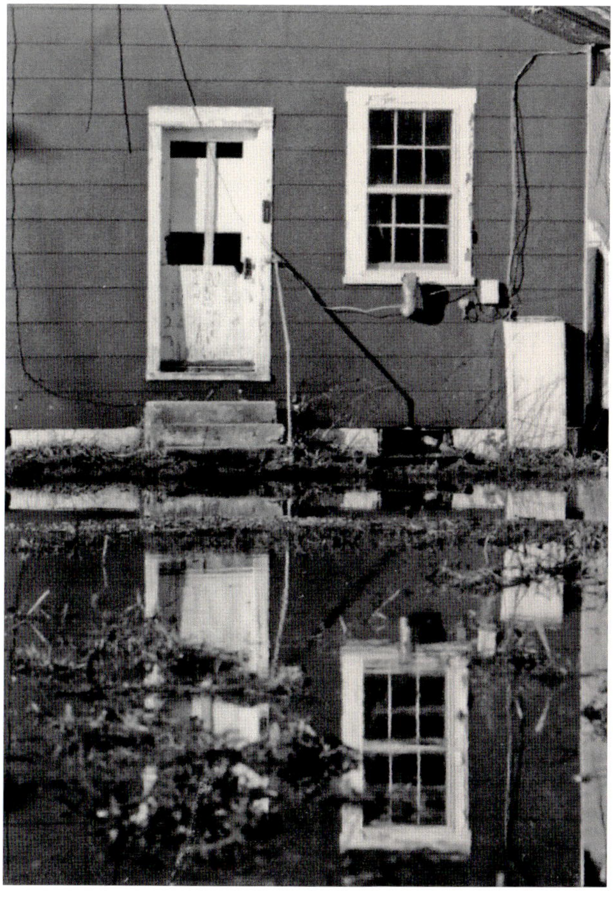

Worcester Fertilizer was also damaged in one of the floods in Snow Hill. The flood of February 1979 put Snow Hill under water for four days and was a result of the 1979 blizzard. There have only been a few times the waters have risen that high. The Worcester Fertilizer Company building has been remodeled and is used by the Worcester County extension office. (Then photograph courtesy of Worcester County Library; now photograph by the author.)

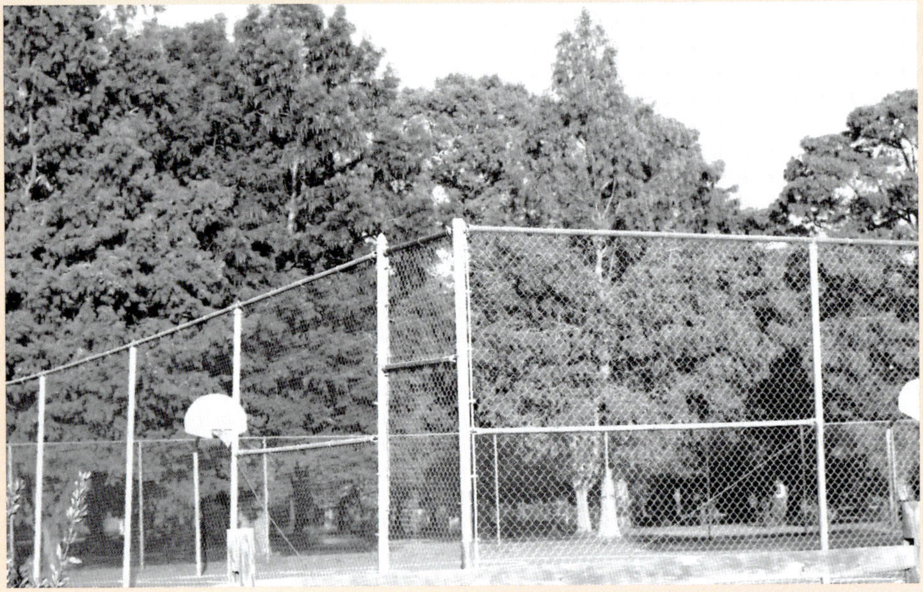

The tennis courts at Byrd Park are shown in the picture below under floodwaters from the 1979 blizzard snowmelt. The tennis courts are still included in the park, and baskets for basketball have been installed. (Then photograph courtesy of Worcester County Library; now photograph by the author.)

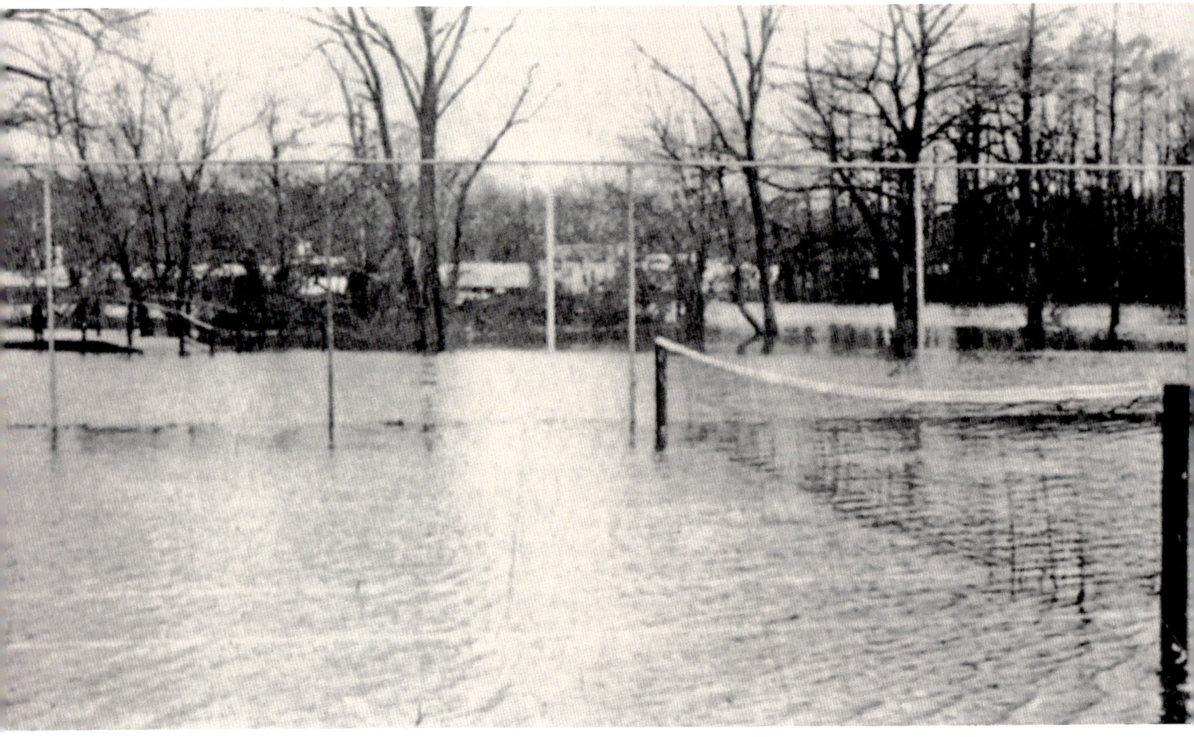

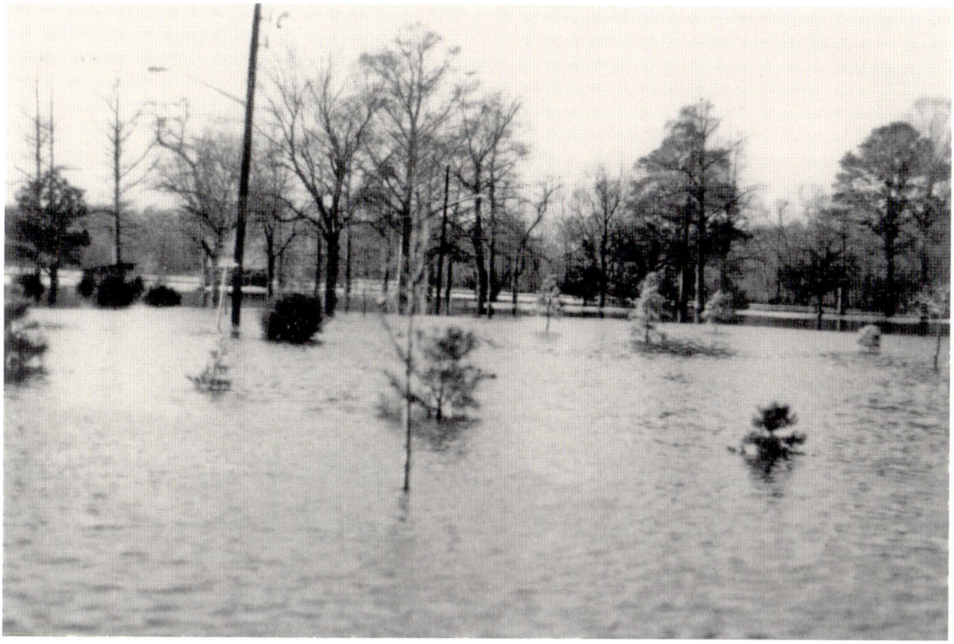

Byrd Park was under water for many days after the snow melted in 1979. The whole waterfront area in Snow Hill was under water, and roadways were shut down. Today Byrd Park is used for many different reasons, including fairs and community programs. (Then photograph courtesy of Worcester County Library; now photograph by the author.)

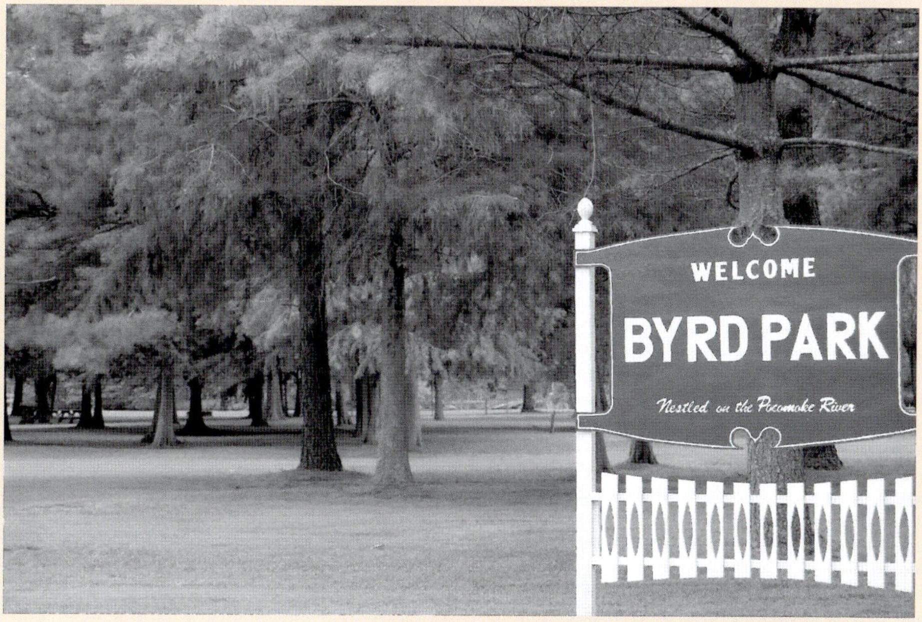

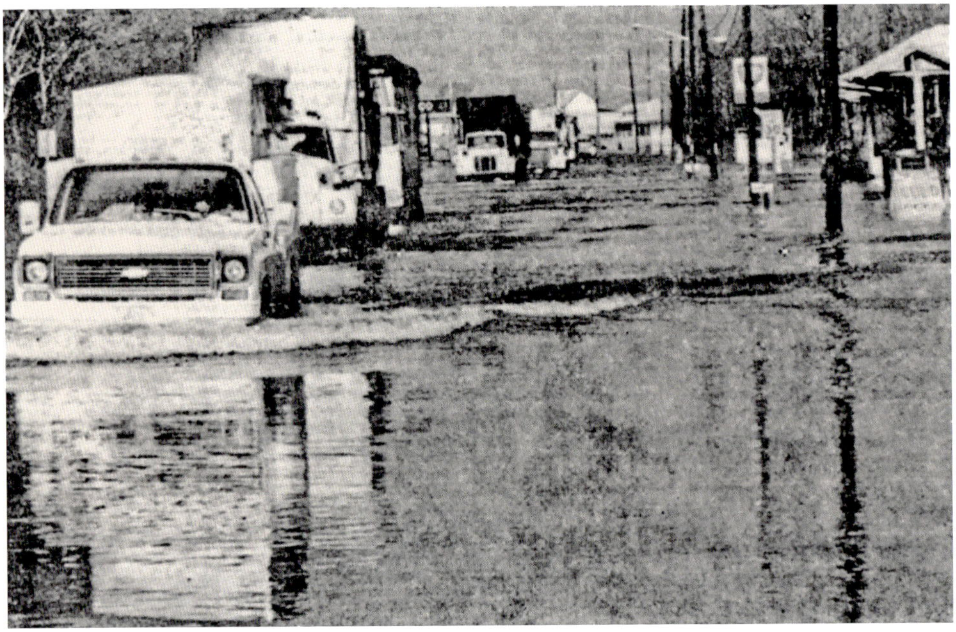

Above, Trucks are shown driving through water that is 36 inches deep after the river rose in 1979. Route 12 was shut down for three days prior to this newspaper picture. Today Route 12 is still one of two maintained ways into Snow Hill. (Then photograph courtesy of Worcester County Library; now photograph by the author.)

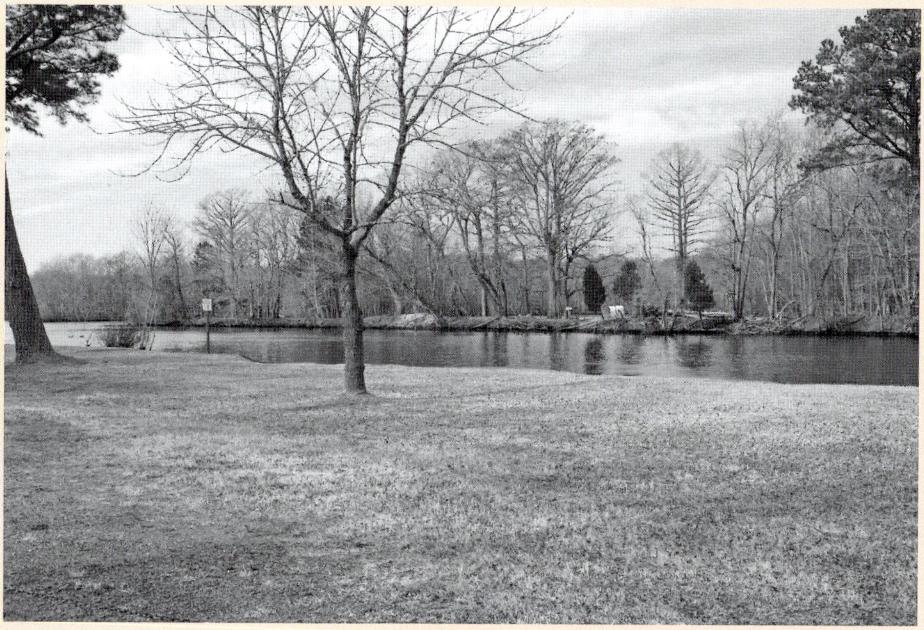

The Timmons mansion, on the banks of the Pocomoke River, burned in 1910. This beautifully constructed home (*c.* 1800, *c.* 1835) featured two-story wraparound porches. This property was owned by Capt. William E. Timmons, who lived in the house until 1902, when he died. The Timmons mansion no longer exists. Nothing has been built in its place. (Then photograph courtesy of Worcester County Library; now photograph by the author.)

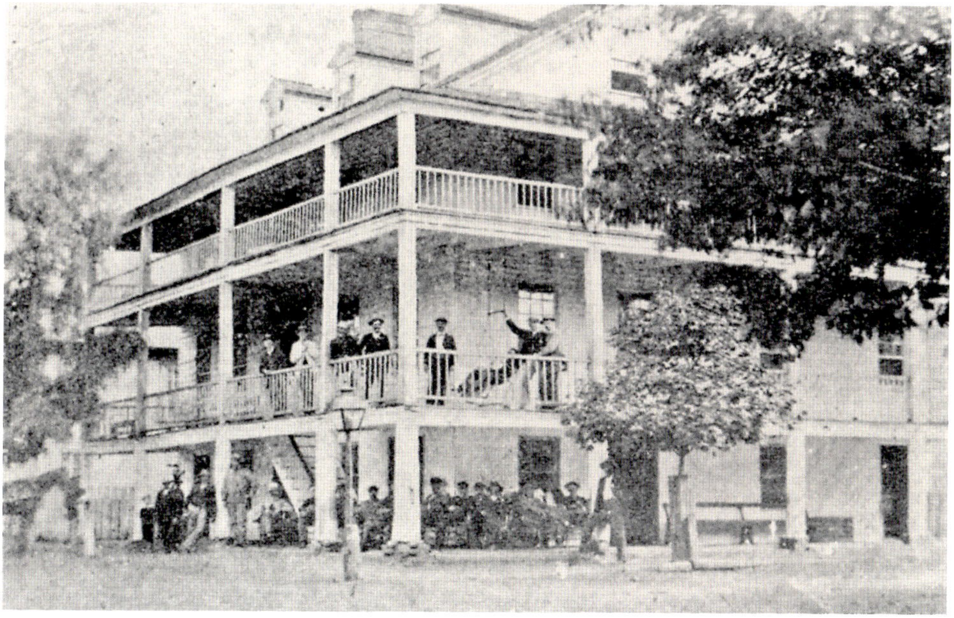